Vocational Business

+ *Financial Accounting*

Roger Lewis & Roger Trevitt

Published in 2003 by:
Nelson Thornes Ltd
Delta Place
27 Bath Road
CHELTENHAM
GL53 7TH
United Kingdom

03 04 05 06 07 / 10 9 8 7 6 5 4 3 2 1

A catalogue record for this book is available from the British Library
ISBN 0 7487 7110 7

Illustrations by Ian West and Steve Ballinger

Page make-up by GreenGate Publishing Services

Printed and bound in Croatia by Zrinski

Contents

Introduction to Vocational Business series

This textbook is one of a series covering the core areas of business studies. The first six books in the series cover the core units of the Business AVCE. A further five books look at the most popular optional units. Each book focuses on vocational aspects of business, rather than theoretical models, allowing the reader to understand how businesses operate. To complement this vocational focus, each book contains a range of case studies illustrating how businesses respond to internal and external changes.

The textbooks are designed to support students taking a range of business courses. While each is free standing, containing the essential knowledge required by the various syllabuses and course requirements, together they provide a comprehensive coverage of the issues facing both large and small businesses in today's competitive environment.

Titles in the series

Book 1   Business at Work
Book 2   The Competitive Business Environment
Book 3   Marketing
Book 4   Human Resources
Book 5   Finance
Book 6   Business Planning

Optional Units: Financial Accounting
**   Market Research**
**   Marketing and Promotional Strategy**
**   Training and Development**
**   Business and the European Union**

Acknowledgements

The authors would like to thank the following people for their support and encouragement with this text: the team at Nelson Thornes, in particular Jane Cotter, Clare Wheelwright and Fiona Elliott, and Liz Brereton at GreenGate; our colleagues and students; and finally to our families once again.

The authors and publishers would also like to thank the following people and organisations for permission to reproduce photographs and other material:
HM Customs and Excise; BACS; Carlton Television Ltd; Toby Melville/Press Association; London Stock Exchange Plc; Inland Revenue.

Every effort has been made to contact copyright holders, and we apologise if any have been overlooked.

Financial Accounting

Introduction

Financial Accounting is offered as an optional unit for AVCE Business by two awarding bodies: Edexcel (Unit 12) and OCR (Unit 11). In each case the unit is internally assessed through portfolio evidence.

Financial Accounting may be taken as part of:
- the AVCE 6 unit award – the vocational 'A' level. In this case the award will comprise compulsory units 1–5 plus the optional unit Financial Accounting
- the AVCE 12 unit double award. Here the award will comprise compulsory units 1–6 plus six optional units including Financial Accounting.

The awarding body evidence requirements are similar but not identical:

Table 1 *Awarding body evidence requirements*

Evidence	Edexcel	OCR
The purpose of keeping financial records	✓	✕ not required
Double-entry book-keeping to trial balance	✓	✓
Adjustments to trial balance	✓	✓
Preparation of final accounts	✓ sole trader, partnership, limited company, non profit-making organisations	✓ limited company published accounts only
Accounting concepts and conventions	✓	✓
Regulation of the accounting process requirements for published accounts only	✓	✓ legal
Computerised accounting	✓	✕ not required

The awarding bodies emphasise different aspects in their portfolio requirements. Whereas Edexcel seeks a broad understanding of accounts for sole traders, partnerships, limited companies and non profit-making organisations, OCR focuses in some depth on the published accounts of limited companies.

In this text we cover the range of evidence requirements. We also provide practise activities and sample assessment materials. The unit assessment is wide ranging and therefore may be best attempted in stages. Financial Accounting is a logical extension of the compulsory Unit 5 Business Finance, and there is necessarily some overlap with this unit. We do not, however, assume that the student is already knowledgeable about this subject; key terms are explained in the margin at relevant stages.

Our aim here has been to provide a flexible resource. We explain, illustrate and practise each stage of the book-keeping and financial reporting process but do not prescribe any particular order of delivery. We recognise that teachers will favour a variety of (equally successful) approaches to this subject. Accordingly we have structured the sections of the book so that they may be attempted in any sequence.

What is financial accounting?

Financial accounting is concerned with recording data from financial documents, and organising and making this information available to stakeholders when it is needed. There is:

- book-keeping – this involves keeping full and accurate financial records of day-to-day transactions.
- accounting – this involves using the business books to produce reports on a company's financial performance for use by its managers and external stakeholders. Such reports include the profit & loss account and the balance sheet.

See Figure 1 opposite. (Stages 1–4 are book-keeping, Stage 5 is accounting.)

Why do businesses need to keep financial records?

A business will keep financial records in order to:

- provide the information that managers need in order to run the business effectively
- satisfy statutory (i.e. legal) requirements.

Management information – used by internal stakeholders to run the business

Those who run the business are called internal stakeholders. They include:

- owners such as sole traders and partners – who will take an active part in running their own businesses
- company directors – who run a company on behalf of the shareholders who own it
- managers – whose jobs are to put policies into effect
- other employees who carry out instructions from managers.

> **Key term**
>
> **Stakeholders** are those who have a legitimate interest in the business and therefore a right to information about it.

> **Key terms**
>
> In accounting, the terms **purchases** and **sales** have a specific meaning:
> - purchases = purchases of stock for resale
> - sales = sales of this stock.

> The first book on double-entry book-keeping was written by Luca Pacioli, an Italian Franciscan monk. It was printed on 10 November 1494.
>
> Pacioli did not invent the system but simply described a method used by merchants at the time. The system included journals and ledgers with asset, liability, capital, income, and expense accounts. He proposed that a trial balance be used to provide a balanced ledger. As we will see, all of these are part of present-day accounting systems.

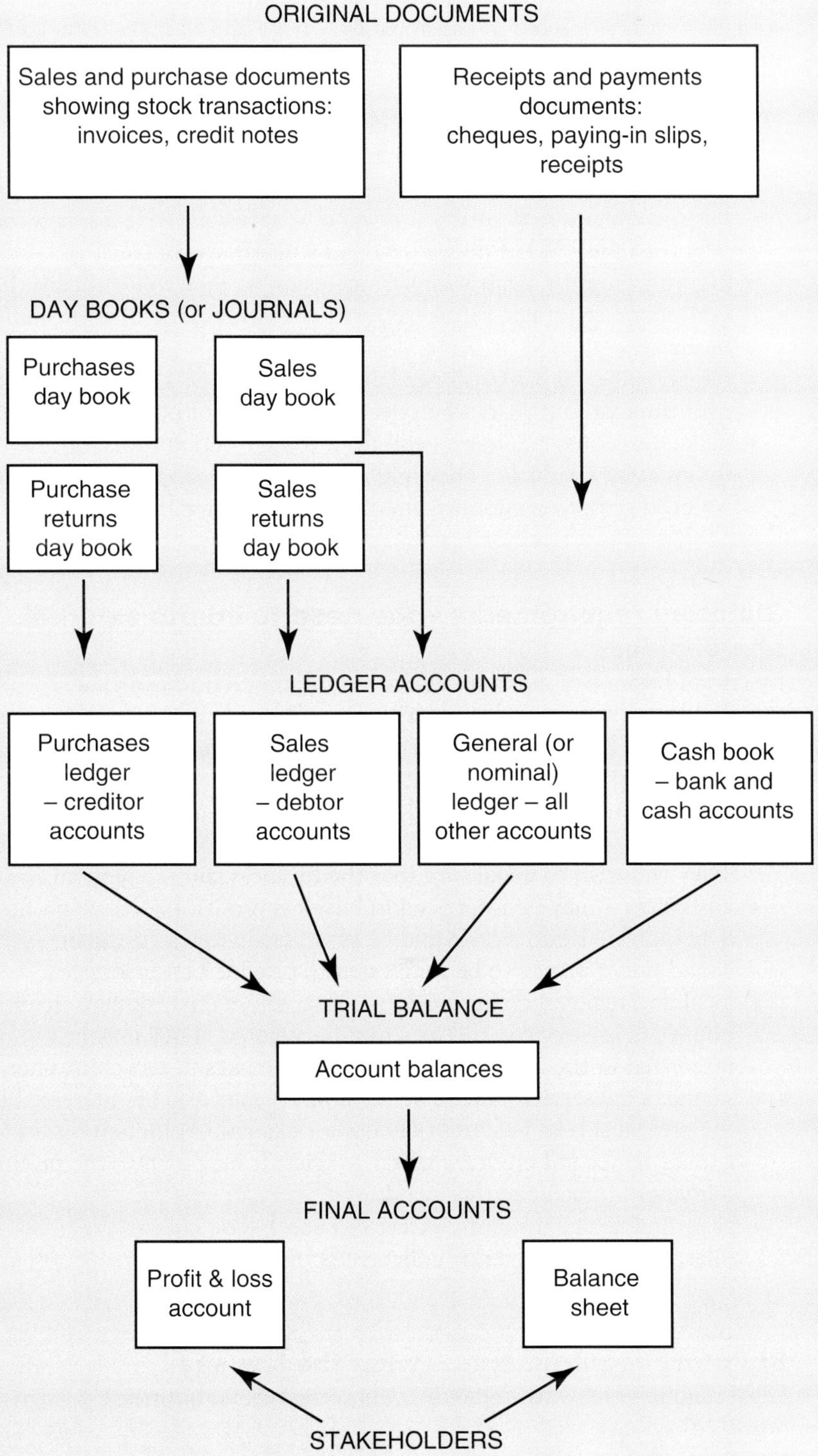
ORIGINAL DOCUMENTS
Sales and purchase documents showing stock transactions: invoices, credit notes
Receipts and payments documents: cheques, paying-in slips, receipts
DAY BOOKS (or JOURNALS)
Purchases day book
Sales day book
Purchase returns day book
Sales returns day book
LEDGER ACCOUNTS
Purchases ledger – creditor accounts
Sales ledger – debtor accounts
General (or nominal) ledger – all other accounts
Cash book – bank and cash accounts
TRIAL BALANCE
Account balances
FINAL ACCOUNTS
Profit & loss account
Balance sheet
STAKEHOLDERS

STAGE 1
Business documents are the source of all accounting records (see pages 7–8 and 12–13)

STAGE 2
Where purchases and sales of stock are on credit it is usual to enter them first of all in the day books using details from invoices and credit notes (see pages 9–11)

STAGE 3
All financial transactions are recorded by making double entries in the ledger:

- purchases, sales and returns of stock are entered from day book details (see pages 23–24)
- receipts and payments use details from cheques, paying-in slips, etc. (see pages 15–17)

STAGE 4
A trial balance is drawn up periodically to check the accuracy of the ledger entries (see pages 19–20)

STAGE 5
Final accounts use accounting records to report the profit/losses for the period and the current value of the business:

- These are used internally by managers
- By law they must be drawn up at the end of each financial year to inform external stakeholders (see pages 36–37)

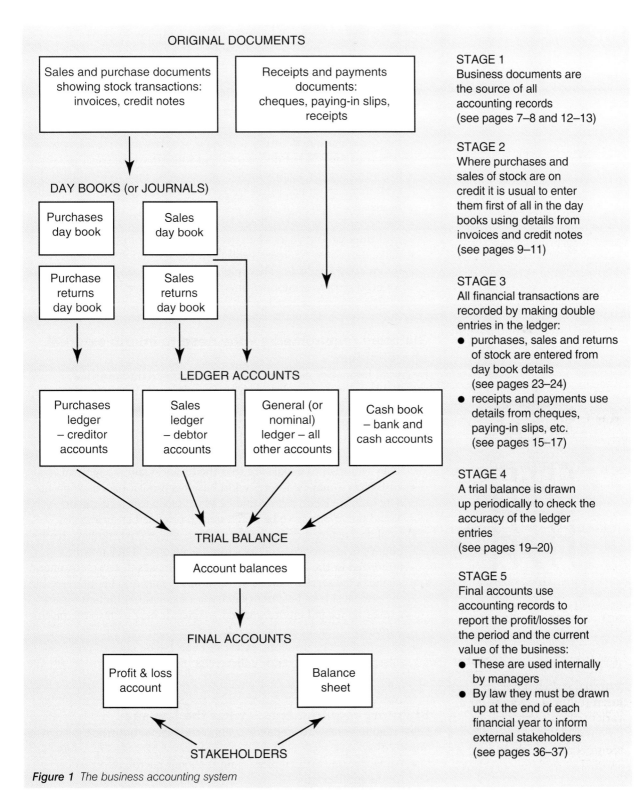

Figure 1 *The business accounting system*

The main financial aims of business management are to generate sufficient cash to enable the business to survive and to make sufficient profit to reward the owners.

The exact management requirements will vary with the type and size of the business; however, managers may use financial records to:

- assess the daily financial position of the business. For example they might ask: what are the sales this week? What are the costs? Who owes us money, how much and when will they pay? How much cash is in the bank? What do we owe and when must we pay?
- monitor progress against targets, for example they will compare the performance (profits, sales, etc.) with previous years, or with similar businesses
- raise finance – a bank will need evidence of business performance over three or four years when deciding whether or not to lend money
- make decisions – managers will need to take action based on the information available. They might ask: do we need to cut costs? Do we need to borrow money? Should we close down this department?

Statutory requirements – the need to inform external shareholders

By law all businesses must disclose some information to external stakeholders. External stakeholders include:

- company shareholders – who are interested in making profits on their investment
- potential investors – who will invest if business performance is good
- creditors – including suppliers who are owed money by the business. They will wish to make sure that the business can repay them
- customers – may be interested in business profits. Excessive profits may indicate that prices could be lower. Sometimes customers would prefer profits to be reinvested to provide better services
- local and regional communities – those whose environment, health, house prices, services and jobs may be affected. They may be interested in the investment the business makes in recycling, energy saving, local services, etc. The community may also be interested in the ethical side of business policies, for example in human rights, animal rights and environmental policies. It may wish to see profits reinvested to achieve these ends
- government departments – Customs and Excise collects VAT on sales, the Inland Revenue collects tax on profits.

Statutory requirements – what the law says

Legal requirements vary depending upon the type of business organisation:

- All businesses with employees must submit payroll information to the Inland Revenue.

Customs and Excise logo

> **Note!**
>
> External stakeholders are interested in a business for a variety of different reasons. Frequently their interests are in conflict with one another.

- All businesses registered for VAT (value added tax) must submit a quarterly VAT return to Customs and Excise (yearly for small businesses).
- All businesses must submit a profit & loss account and balance sheet to the Inland Revenue at the end of the financial year so that tax can be calculated. (If annual turnover is below £15,000 detailed accounts are not required.)

Other than these requirements, sole traders and partnerships are able to keep their accounts private, although they may wish to show them to banks and other investors when raising finance.

Limited companies, on the other hand, are required by the Companies Acts of 1985 and 1989 to publish their final accounts, i.e. to make them public, by lodging a copy at Companies House.

The main reasons for the additional regulation of limited companies are that:

- they have unlimited liability so there is a need to protect creditors and potential investors who may not be repaid if the company fails
- they are run by directors but owned by the shareholders. The shareholders need to know that the directors are performing their duty of 'stewardship', i.e. they are using shareholders' funds wisely
- large companies are also likely to affect the lives of a wide number of people. The external stakeholders we have mentioned are more likely to be concerned with the activities of companies than sole traders or partnerships which tend to be small.

Large companies are required to have their accounts audited, i.e. checked to ensure that stakeholders are not being misled. The Enron case study (pages 75–76) shows that auditors do not always find the truth.

Ⓒ ASE STUDY

Railtrack

The directors of a company must serve the interests of the various stakeholders. However, there may be a conflict between:

- the duty of stewardship they owe to the shareholders and
- the duty they have to other stakeholders.

When the rail network was privatised in 1996, the regional rail services were franchised to different companies such as Connex, Virgin and GNER. Railtrack, a profit-making plc, was set up to maintain the infrastructure (the track, stations and other property). Shares were sold to the general public and to city investors. At first the share price rose, but then came a series of rail disasters. The company came under criticism for paying dividends to shareholders rather than investing in a safer and more effective rail service.

The share price fell as it became clear that the company was in financial difficulties. More investment was needed but the government

---

Key terms

The **profit & loss** account and **balance sheet** = the **final accounts**.

Companies Acts and Companies House, page 75

Key term

Unlimited liability means that company shareholders will not lose their private wealth if their company fails. The most they will lose is the cash they have invested or promised to invest.

Key term

Stewardship permits the directors of a company to be entrusted with shareholders' money. They must use it wisely and try to generate a satisfactory profit for them.

was unwilling to help in a situation where funds were as likely to go to shareholders as to improvements in safety. Shareholders were unlikely to invest with prospects looking so uncertain.

In 2002 Railtrack was put into administration by Stephen Byers, the transport secretary at the time. The company was regarded as insolvent – although there was some disagreement about this – and was put into administration until it could be restructured.

Finally a deal was struck. Shareholders would gain some compensation and a new not-for-profit company called Network Rail was set up to take over Railtrack's responsibilities.

Tasks

1 Who were the stakeholders in Railtrack? Why might each wish to see the final accounts?
2 Identify any conflicts of interest that the directors might encounter in serving the various stakeholders.

The consequences of keeping inaccurate accounts

Management and statutory requirements can only be met properly if financial records are accurate. The consequences of inaccurate records might include:

- inappropriate management decisions, e.g. if managers think a profit is being made when it is a loss they will not realise there is a problem
- incorrect customer statements or late payment to suppliers. This could lead to loss of customers, or suppliers being unwilling to give credit
- legal action being taken by the Inland Revenue or Customs and Excise
- the reputation of the business being damaged if auditors do not believe the accounts give a true and fair view. Future investors may be put off investing in the company.

ACTIVITY

Write a report under the heading:
The purpose and value of keeping accurate financial records
You should mention:

- the business accounting system
- statutory reporting requirements
- disclosure of information
- stakeholder information requirements
- the need for accuracy.

- management information requirements
- Companies House
- limited liability
- stewardship

You should follow up the cross references to other related sections within the book for further information.

| Recording financial transactions

Original documents

Each financial transaction has an original document. The main documents used for book-keeping entries are: invoices, credit notes, cheques, paying-in slips and receipts.

Invoices

Invoices are sales and purchases documents. They indicate the payment due when we buy or sell goods on credit.

The invoice below is a sales invoice from the point of view of World Cups the supplier, but a purchase invoice for JJ Ltd the customer.

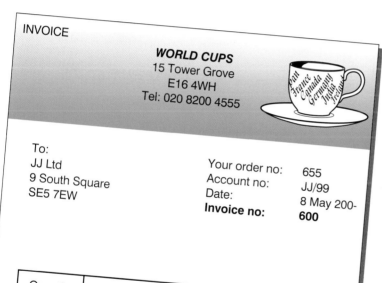

<table>
<tr><td colspan="3">

Key terms

A **purchases invoice** is received from a supplier (or creditor). It shows how much we owe for a particular purchase.
A **sales invoice** is sent to a customer (or debtor). It shows how much the customer owes us.

</td></tr>
</table>

INVOICE

WORLD CUPS
15 Tower Grove
E16 4WH
Tel: 020 8200 4555

To:
JJ Ltd
9 South Square
SE5 7EW

Your order no: 655
Account no: JJ/99
Date: 8 May 200-
Invoice no: **600**

Quantity	Details	Unit price £	Total £
2 doz 16 doz	Bavarian 500ml Tokyo (wide rim)	£16.00 doz £8.00 doz	32.00 128.00
	VAT @ 17.5% TOTAL DUE	160.00 28.00 188.00	

Terms: strictly net settlement within 30 days of invoice

WORLD CUPS 15 Tower Grove E16 4WH
Tel: 020 8200 4555

Figure 2 *Invoice example*

Credit notes

Credit notes reduce the charge on a particular invoice, perhaps because goods have been overcharged or returned.

The credit note below is a sales credit note from the point of view of World Cups the supplier but a purchase credit note for JJ Ltd the customer.

Recording invoices and credit notes

Document	Day book where details are listed
Purchases invoices	Purchases day book
Sales invoices	Sales day book
Purchases credit notes	Purchases returns day book
Sales credit notes	Sales returns day book

CREDIT NOTE

WORLD CUPS
15 Tower Grove
E16 4WH
Tel: 020 8200 4555

To:
JJ Ltd
9 South Square
SE5 7EW

Our invoice no: 600
Account no: JJ/99
Date: 17 May 200-
Credit note no: C10

Quantity	Details	Unit Price £	Total £
2 doz	Tokyo (wide rim)	£8.00 doz	16.00
			16.00
	VAT @ 17.5%		2.80
	TOTAL CREDIT		18.80

Goods returned as faulty

WORLD CUPS 15 Tower Grove E16 4WH
Tel: 020 8200 4555

Figure 3 Credit note example

VAT (value added tax)

Most businesses are registered for VAT because their annual sales exceed the registration threshold set by the government. This means that they must charge VAT on their sales (output tax), but it also enables them to claim back the VAT paid when they buy goods and services (input tax). For this reason they must record VAT separately in the day books. Later this will be transferred to the VAT account.

 VAT account, page 24

The day books (or journals) – recording purchases, sales and returns

Where a business buys and sells on credit, invoices and credit notes are entered into day books as a first stage in the recording process.

For example, World Cups buys and sells on credit. The following example shows how invoices and credit notes for May are entered into the day books.

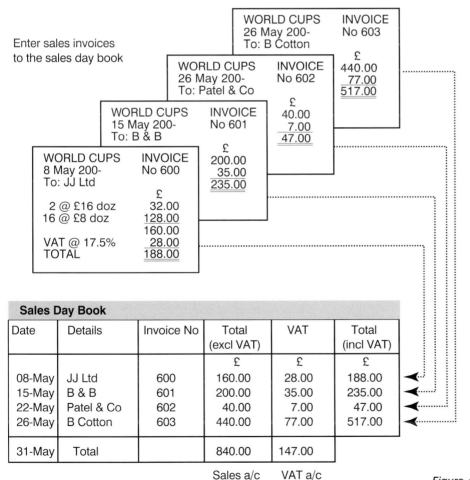

Enter sales invoices to the sales day book

WORLD CUPS	INVOICE	
26 May 200-	No 603	
To: B Cotton		
		£
		440.00
		77.00
		517.00

WORLD CUPS	INVOICE	
26 May 200-	No 602	
To: Patel & Co		
		£
		40.00
		7.00
		47.00

WORLD CUPS	INVOICE	
15 May 200-	No 601	
To: B & B		
		£
		200.00
		35.00
		235.00

WORLD CUPS	INVOICE	
8 May 200-	No 600	
To: JJ Ltd		
		£
2 @ £16 doz		32.00
16 @ £8 doz		128.00
		160.00
VAT @ 17.5%		28.00
TOTAL		188.00

Sales Day Book

Date	Details	Invoice No	Total (excl VAT)	VAT	Total (incl VAT)
			£	£	£
08-May	JJ Ltd	600	160.00	28.00	188.00
15-May	B & B	601	200.00	35.00	235.00
22-May	Patel & Co	602	40.00	7.00	47.00
26-May	B Cotton	603	440.00	77.00	517.00
31-May	Total		840.00	147.00	
			Sales a/c	VAT a/c	

Figure 4 Recording credit sales

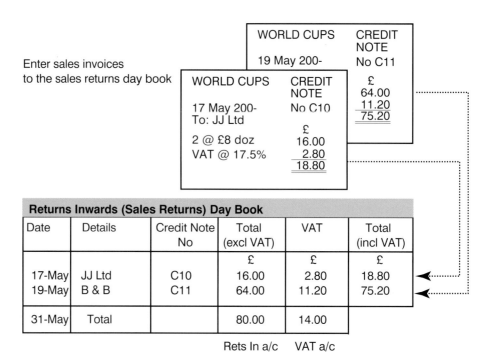

Enter sales invoices to the sales returns day book

Returns Inwards (Sales Returns) Day Book

Date	Details	Credit Note No	Total (excl VAT)	VAT	Total (incl VAT)
			£	£	£
17-May	JJ Ltd	C10	16.00	2.80	18.80
19-May	B & B	C11	64.00	11.20	75.20
31-May	Total		80.00	14.00	

Rets In a/c   VAT a/c

Figure 5 Recording sales returns

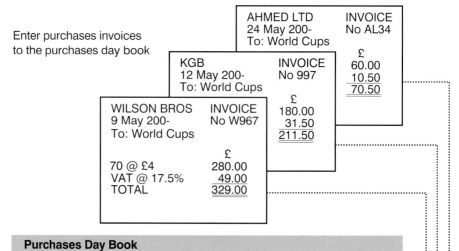

Enter purchases invoices to the purchases day book

Purchases Day Book

Date	Details	Invoice No	Total (excl VAT)	VAT	Total (incl VAT)
			£	£	£
09-May	Wilson Bros	W967	280.00	49.00	329.00
12-May	KGB	997	180.00	31.50	211.50
24-May	Ahmed Ltd	AL34	60.00	10.50	70.50
31-May	Total		520.00	91.00	

Purchases   VAT a/c

Figure 6 Recording credit purchases

Enter purchase credit notes to the purchase returns day book

```
                          AHMED LTD        CREDIT
                          29 May 200-      NOTE
                          To: World Cups   No C05
          KGB                CREDIT           £
          18 May 200-        NOTE          32.00
          To: World Cups   No CA12          5.60
                                           37.60
                              £
          2 @ £4            8.00
          VAT @ 17.5%       1.40
                            9.40
```

Returns Outwards (Purchase Returns) Day Book

Date	Details	Credit Note No	Total (excl VAT)	VAT	Total (incl VAT)
			£	£	£
18-May	KGB	CA12	8.00	1.40	9.40
29-May	Ahmed Ltd	C05	32.00	5.60	37.60
31-May	Total		40.00	7.00	

Rets Out a/c   VAT a/c

Figure 7 *Recording purchase returns*

Day books to ledger accounts, page 22

What happens to the day book details?

The day books are books of original entry for transactions involving credit purchases, sales and returns of stock. Later on we will see how details from these day books are entered into the business accounts.

ACTIVITY

You work for Guy Roper (Camping Supplies). Details of purchase and sales documents for March are as follows:

3 March   Sent sales invoice no 1322 to Hiking & Biking (customer):
          £400 excl VAT + £70 VAT
5 March   Received purchase invoice no 453 from Mistral (supplier):
          £600 excl VAT + £105 VAT
8 March   Sent sales invoice no 1323 to Windjammer Ltd (customer):
          £800 excl VAT + £140 VAT
9 March   Sent sales invoice no 1324 to Gales & Co (customer):
          £80 excl VAT + £14 VAT
12 March Received purchase credit note no CN56 from Mistral for faulty
          goods returned: £120 excl VAT + £21 VAT
14 March Sent sales credit note no C345 to Windjammer Ltd:
          £40 excl VAT + £7 VAT for faulty goods returned
15 March Received purchase invoice no 214 from Top Tents (supplier):
          £1,200 excl VAT + £210 VAT

21 March	Received purchase invoice no 789 from Hardy Ridgepole (supplier): £1,560 excl VAT+ £273 VAT
23 March	Sent sales invoice no 1325 to Arctic Bedrolls (customer): £2,400 excl VAT+ £420 VAT
27 March	Sent sales credit note no C346 to Arctic Bedrolls: £200 excl VAT+ £35 VAT for faulty goods returned
30 March	Received purchase credit note no C223 from Hardy Ridgepole for faulty goods returned: £240 excl VAT+ £42 VAT

Tasks

1 Rule up the purchase day book, purchases returns day book, sales day book and sales returns day book. Enter up details for the month.
2 Total all day books at the month end.

The answers to this appear in the activity on page 25.

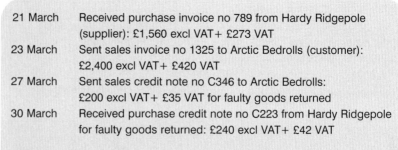

Receipts and payments documents

A variety of methods may be used for paying money and each has its own documentation:

- cash (i.e. physical notes and coins) – a receipt must be issued because there is no other document to verify the payment
- cheques – the transaction will be recorded on the bank statement; the chequebook counterfoil also shows cheque details
- direct payments through the banking system by standing order, direct debit, credit transfer (Giro) and BACS (bankers automated clearing system)
- card transactions – debit and credit card purchases
- paying-in slips are used when depositing cash, cheques, credit card vouchers, etc. into the bank. Ultimately, the bank statement will record the deposit, but the counterfoil should be kept as a receipt.

The cheque below is a receipt document from the point of view of JM Properties, the payee, and a payment for the drawer World Cups.

Figure 8 Cheque example

The paying-in slip below is a receipt document for World Cups, into whose bank account the money has been paid.

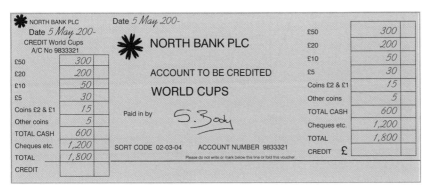

Figure 9 Paying-in slip example

 The cheque and paying-in slip are recorded on the cash book of World Cups on page 15.

ACTIVITY

You work for a mail order supplier, Stationery to Go! All transactions are on credit.

1 Which business document will you send to your customer in each of the following situations?
   a) You sell photocopying paper to a customer.
   b) Your customer returns some of this paper as it is damaged.
2 Which business document will you receive from your supplier in each of the following situations?
   a) You buy 400 folders from a supplier.
   b) You return 50 of these as the fasteners are faulty.
3 Which documents confirm details of the following?
   a) A cheque sent to your supplier.
   b) Cash and cheques deposited in the business bank account.

Key terms

Ledger accounts record:
- **assets** – items of value that the business owns, e.g. premises, vehicles, bank balance
- **liabilities** – money the business owes to others, e.g. bank loan, creditors
- **incomes** – sales being the main example
- **expenses** – day to day costs such as rent, wages, salaries and heating
- **capital** – funds invested by the owner(s), i.e. the sole trader, the partners or (in a company) the shareholders
- **drawings** – funds taken out by the sole trader or partners (in a company the shareholders are paid dividends).

Debtors who owe the business money are **assets**.
Creditors who are owed money by the business are **liabilities**.

The ledger accounts –
double-entry book-keeping

The details from the business documents will need to be entered into the business accounts, known as the ledger. Receipts and payments are entered directly, credits and purchases via the day books.

The ledger accounts are grouped into three (or sometimes four) sections (see Figure 10, page 14).

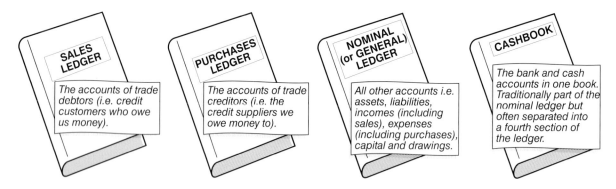

Figure 10 Ledger accounts

Debits and credits

Each ledger account has two sides:
- the debit side (left-hand side) – an entry here records value coming into the account
- the credit side (right-hand side) – an entry here records value going out of the account.

Table 2 The two sides of a ledger account

IN – RECEIVES VALUE			OUT – GIVES VALUE		
Debit		Account name			**Credit**
Date	Details	£	Date	Details	£
date of transaction	account where value came from	value in	date of transaction	account where value has gone	money out

Each entry records three items of information:
- the transaction date
- the value of the transaction
- the detail – each transaction affects two accounts (there is a 'double entry'). The name of the other account goes here.

> **Note!**
>
> The ledger accounts are sometimes called 'T' accounts because of their shape.

Making ledger entries – recording receipts and payments in the cash book

The cash book records all money received and paid. For now we assume that all receipts and payments are bank transactions so that our cashbook is the business bank account only.

World Cups began trading on 1 May. Our job is to enter up the business cash book for the period 1–7 May.

The cash book may have separate columns for cash and bank transactions, see pages 26–28.

Table 3 *World Cups cash book entries, 1–7 May*

Date	Transaction	Cash book (bank account) entries	
		Receipt debit	Payment credit
1 May	Opened a business bank account by paying in £10,000 of our own savings (capital a/c)	✓	
2 May	Paid rent of £1,000		✓
3 May	Bought a van for £2,000 (van a/c)		✓
4 May	Bought stock for £600 (purchases a/c)		✓
5 May	Sold stock for £1,800 (sales a/c)	✓	
6 May	Borrowed £500 (loan)	✓	
7 May	Bought more stock for £400 (purchases a/c)		✓

Key term

Capital = funds invested in the business by the owner(s), i.e. a sole trader, partners or company shareholders.

The cash book will appear like this:

Table 4 *World Cups cash book (bank account)*

Dr						Cr
Date	Details	£	Date	Details	£	
1 May	Capital	10,000	2 May	Rent	1,000	
5 May	Sales	1,800	3 May	Van	2,000	
6 May	Loan	500	4 May	Purchases	600	
			7 May	Purchases	400	

Key terms

Remember that the **purchases account** is only used when we buy stock for resale and the **sales account** is only used when we sell this stock.
When we buy or sell an asset such as the van we use the asset account.

ACTIVITY

Les Routier has just set up a transport cafe. All receipts and payments pass through the bank account.

Note!

Recording sales and purchases of stock
- Where sales and purchases are on credit we use day books, see pages 9–11
- Where sales and purchases are for cash (immediate payment) we record them directly to the cash book, see page 14.

Task

Your job is to rule up the cash book and enter the transactions for June:

1 June	Capital of £8,000 paid into the business bank account
2 June	A loan of £2,000 paid into the business bank account
4 June	Paid rent of £2,000 by cheque
5 June	Bought equipment for £7,000 paid by cheque
	Bought a van for £1,500 paid for by cheque
6 June	Les withdrew £300 for his own use (drawings a/c)
8 June	Purchased stocks for £1,450 paid for by cheque
10 June	£850 paid into the bank from sales of stock
11 June	Wrote a cheque for £25 for petrol
15 June	Sales of £910 paid into the bank
16 June	Les withdrew £300 for his own use (drawings a/c)

Double-entry book-keeping

Two ledger entries (a double entry) are needed to record each transaction, so each time we debit the cash book (because it receives) we must credit the account which gives this value.

For example, the cash book for World Cups is shown again below, this time accompanied by the double entries in the ledger. The double entry for 1 May has been highlighted. See if you can trace the other double entries. Remember that the details column tells where the double entry is to be found.

Dr		**Cash book (bank account)**			Cr
Date	Details	£	Date	Details	£
1 May	Capital	10,000	2 May	Rent	1,000
5 May	Sales	1,800	3 May	Van	2,000
6 May	Loan	500	4 May	Purchases	600
			7 May	Purchases	400

Dr		**Capital**			Cr
Date	Details	£	Date	Details	£
			1 May	bank	10,000

Dr		**Rent**			Cr
Date	Details	£	Date	Details	£
2 May	Bank	1,000			

Dr		**Van**			Cr
Date	Details	£	Date	Details	£
3 May	Bank	2,000			

Cont'd

Dr			**Purchases**		Cr
Date	Details	£	Date	Details	£
4 May	Bank	600			
7 May	Bank	400			

Dr			**Sales**		Cr
Date	Details	£	Date	Details	£
			5 May	Bank	1,800

Dr			**Loan**		Cr
Date	Details	£	Date	Details	£
			6 May	Bank	500

Figure 11 Double-entry book-keeping

CTIVITY

Make sure that you have completed the cash book for Les Routier from the previous activity. Now rule up the necessary accounts and complete the double entries.

Balancing an account

Ledger accounts are balanced periodically, perhaps weekly or monthly, to find out the state of each account. The balance on an account is simply the difference in value between the two sides.

For example, the cash book of World Cups would be balanced like this:

1 Total each side of the account. In the example:
   Debit total = £12,300 (£10,000 + £1,800 + £500)
   Credit total = £4,000 (£1,000 + £2,000 + £600 + £400).
2 Calculate the balance (the difference between the totals):
   £12,300 – £4,000 = £8,300.
3 Enter the balance at the bottom of the smaller side – in this case the credit side. Call this 'balance c/d' meaning balance to be carried down.
4 Now the two sides will have equal totals. Enter these totals in line with each other and draw a double line beneath each one.
5 Bring down the balance to the opposite side (in this case the debit side) on the next working day. Call this 'balance b/d' meaning balance brought down.

> **Key terms**
>
> **balance c/d** = balance to be carried down
> **balance b/d** = balance brought down
> Each new period begins with the balance b/d.

 Zero balances, page 29

> **Note!**
>
> If the debit and credit totals are equal then the balance is zero and is not shown. On page 29 customer JJ Ltd has a zero balance; they have settled their account in full.

Dr			**Cash book**		Cr
Date	Details	£	Date	Details	£
1 May	Capital	10,000	2 May	Rent	1,000
5 May	Sales	1,800	3 May	Van	2,000
6 May	Loan	500	4 May	Purchases	600
			7 May	Purchases	400
			7 May	Balance c/d	8,300
		12,300			12,300
8 May	Balance b/d	8,300			

Figure 12 Cash book for World Cups

Debit and credit balances:

- a balance brought down to the debit side of an account is called a debit balance. This happens when the debit side is the larger. The cash book of World Cups (see page 17), has a debit balance of £8,300 on 8th May, showing that there is £8,300 in the bank
- a balance brought down to the credit side is called a credit balance and happens when the credit side is the larger
- a credit balance on the bank account would indicate an overdraft.

The balance brought down is the first entry for the coming period and is a summary of the position at that time.

What does an account balance tell us?

We can classify accounts as personal, real or nominal, and, depending upon the type of account, the balance means something slightly different.

Key term

Real accounts are accounts indicating physical assets owned by the business.

Table 5 An example of a real account

Example	What the balance means	Debit or credit balance
Cash book	How much money is in the bank	All assets are debits
Van	The value of the van (when new)	

Key term

Personal accounts are accounts of people or businesses, i.e. debtors, creditors, liabilities or capital.

Table 6 An example of a personal account

Example	What the balance means	Debit or credit balance
JJ Ltd (debtor)	How much JJ owes us	Debit
Wilson Bros (creditor)	How much we owe Wilson Bros	Credit
Capital (the owner)	How much the business owes to the owner	Credit
Loan (HH Ltd)	How much is owed to the lender	Credit

Key term

Nominal accounts are accounts showing income or expenses.

Table 7 An example of a nominal account

Example	What the balance means	Debit or credit balance
Sales	The value of sales made in the period	Credit
Purchases	The cost of purchases in the period	Debit
Rent	The rent paid in the period	Debit
Drawings	The value taken from the business by the owner(s) in the period	Debit

Balancing accounts and drawing up a trial balance

All of the accounts of World Cups have been balanced at 7 May.

Notice that there are slightly different balancing procedures for each of the following situations:

- accounts have entries on both sides (cash book)
- accounts have more than one entry but all are on the same side (purchases account)
- accounts have only one entry (capital, rent, van, sales and loan accounts).

Dr		Cash book (bank account)				Cr
Date	Details	£	Date	Details		£
1 May	Capital	10,000	2 May	Rent		1,000
5 May	Sales	1,800	3 May	Van		2,000
6 May	Loan	500	4 May	Purchases		600
			7 May	Purchases		400
		12,300	7 May	Balance c/d		12,300
8 May	Balance b/d	8,300				

Dr		Capital			Cr
Date	Details	£	Date	Details	£
7 May	Balance c/d	10,000	1 May	Bank	10,000
			8 May	Balance b/d	10,000

Dr		Rent			Cr
Date	Details	£	Date	Details	£
2 May	Bank	1,000	7 May	Balance c/d	1,000
8 May	Balance b/d	1,000			

Dr		Van			Cr
Date	Details	£	Date	Details	£
3 May	Bank	2,000	7 May	Balance c/d	2,000
8 May	Balance b/d	2,000			

Dr		Purchases			Cr
Date	Details	£	Date	Details	£
4 May	Bank	600			
7 May	Bank	400	7 May	Balance c/d	1,000
		1,000			1,000
8 May	Balance b/d	1,000			

Dr		Sales			Cr
Date	Details	£	Date	Details	£
7 May	Balance c/d	1,800	5 May	Bank	1,800
			8 May	Balance b/d	1,800

Dr		Loan			Cr
Date	Details	£	Date	Details	£
7 May	Balance c/d	500	6 May	Bank	500
			8 May	Balance b/d	500

Figure 13 Drawing up a trial balance

	Debit £	Credit £
Bank	8,300	
Capital		10,000
Rent	1,000	
Van	2,000	
Purchases	1,000	
Sales		1,800
Loan		500
	12,300	12,300

Figure 14 Trial balance of World Cups as at 7 May 200-

Key term

A **trading period** is the period over which business profits are reported. By law a business must report profit or losses at the end of each financial year. For management reasons it may wish to do so more often than this – perhaps each quarter or each month.

Accounting software enables financial reports to be produced whenever they are needed.

The trial balance

At the end of a trading period the book-keeper will balance the ledger accounts and draw up a trial balance: a list of all the balances on the ledger with debit balances and credit balances placed in separate columns and totalled.

The trial balance serves two purposes:

- It is used to check the accuracy of the ledger. Where the trial balance balances (i.e. the debit balances equal the credit balances) then it is assumed that the ledger entries are correct. If there is a difference there is an error and the ledger must be rechecked.
- It provides a convenient list from which the final accounts (the profit & loss account and balance sheet) can be drawn up.

Notice that the balances are arranged as follows:

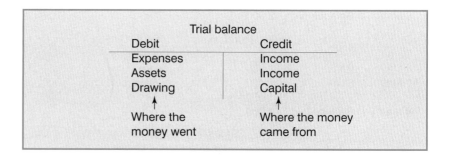

Figure 15 A trial balance

There are often a large number of debtors and creditors on the business books. For this reason a trial balance will usually show total debtors and total creditors rather than individual accounts. The example on pages 97–98 illustrates this.

(A)CTIVITY

Note!

See where the trial balance fits into the accounting process by referring back to Figure 1 on page 3.

Dot's Coms (ladies fashions) has the following account balances on the ledger as at 31 December 200-:

Purchases	£100,000	D
Sales	£180,000	C
Light & heat	£2,000	D
Salaries	£55,000	D
General administration	£12,000	D
Furniture and fittings	£25,000	D
Capital	£20,000	C
Debtors	£1,000	D
Creditors	£2,000	C
Rent & rates	£8,000	D
Bank	£3,000	D
Loan	£4,000	C

Tasks

1 Draw up the trial balance.
   (Hint: classify each item as in Figure 14 on page 20 before you begin.)
2 How will you know if you are correct?

Limitations of the trial balance

In practice the trial balance can only check that the debit entries are equal to the credit entries in the ledger. There are a number of errors that it cannot detect; it will still balance even though these errors have been made:

- errors of omission – a transaction is missed out altogether so that there is neither a debit nor a credit entry, e.g. an invoice might have blown out of the window and no entry at all is made
- errors of principle – a double entry is made but into the wrong class of account. For example petrol should be debited to the motor expenses account but instead is debited into the motor vehicle account (an asset)
- errors of commission – the correct class of account is used but the wrong account is chosen, e.g. a Jones instead of James
- reversal of entries – a consistent double entry is made but the debit and credits are the wrong way round, e.g. debit bank and credit rent when rent is paid (instead of the other way round)
- compensating error – by chance two or more errors cancel themselves out.

Ⓐ CTIVITY

Trial balance of Ali's Barbershop as at 31 December 200-

	Debit £	Credit £
Sales		50,000
Purchases	23,000	
Premises	70,000	
Furniture & fittings		20,000
Vehicles	5,000	
Debtors	800	
Bank	10,000	
Creditors		500
Motor expenses	1,000	
Office expenses	2,200	
Salaries	34,500	
Bank loan		5,000
Capital		60,000
Drawings	18,000	
	150,000	150,000

Task

1 Although the trial balance totals agree there is a problem.
  a) What is it?
  b) Which type of error is most likely to have caused this problem?
  c) Which other account is therefore also likely to be incorrect?
  d) On the trial balance identify each account as either: asset, liability, income, expense, capital or drawings.
  e) Ali's capital account, drawings account, sales account, premises account and motor expenses accounts are all correct. For each one explain what the balance tells us.

2 Frank Marvin has made the following book-keeping errors. Name the type of error in each case:
  a) He sold goods on credit to Max Mart Ltd but debited the account of Max Hart instead.
  b) He bought new office furniture but debited office expenses instead of furniture & fittings.
  c) He mislaid a credit note so no entry was made in the books.

> **Note!**
>
> On pages 16–17 we saw how World Cups recorded receipts and payments in the cashbook with a double entry made to the ledger.
>
> On pages 9–11 we saw how World Cups recorded credit sales, purchases and returns in the day books. Here we show how these are now recorded in the ledger by double entry.

Posting day books to the ledger

Remember that the day books list credit sales, credit purchases and returns of stock.

On pages 23 and 24 we show how to enter these details to the ledger using double-entry book-keeping.

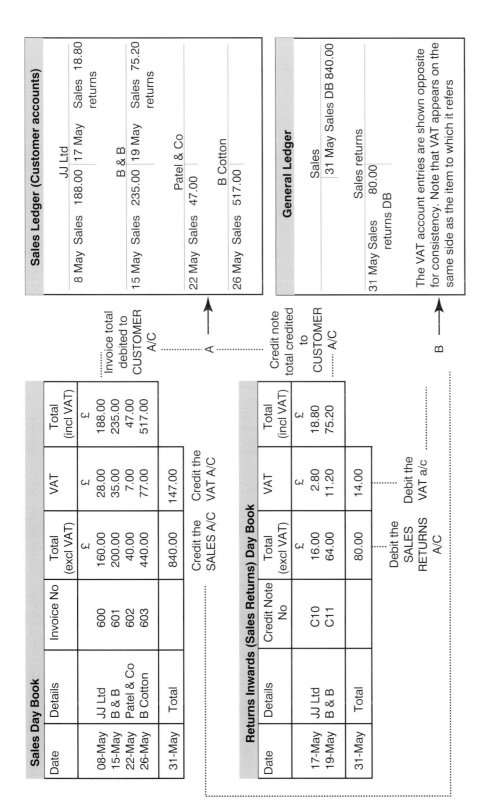

Sales Ledger (Customer accounts)

JJ Ltd

| 8 May Sales 188.00 | 17 May | Sales returns 18.80 |

B & B

| 15 May Sales 235.00 | 19 May | Sales returns 75.20 |

Patel & Co

22 May Sales 47.00

B Cotton

26 May Sales 517.00

General Ledger

Sales

| | 31 May Sales DB 840.00 |

Sales returns

| 31 May Sales returns DB 80.00 | |

The VAT account entries are shown opposite for consistency. Note that VAT appears on the same side as the item to which it refers

Sales Day Book

Date	Details	Invoice No	Total (excl VAT) £	VAT £	Total (incl VAT) £
08-May	JJ Ltd	600	160.00	28.00	188.00
15-May	B & B	601	200.00	35.00	235.00
22-May	Patel & Co	602	40.00	7.00	47.00
26-May	B Cotton	603	440.00	77.00	517.00
31-May	Total		840.00	147.00	

Credit the SALES A/C   Credit the VAT A/C

Invoice total debited to CUSTOMER A/C

A ⟶

Returns Inwards (Sales Returns) Day Book

Date	Details	Credit Note No	Total (excl VAT) £	VAT £	Total (incl VAT) £
17-May	JJ Ltd	C10	16.00	2.80	18.80
19-May	B & B	C11	64.00	11.20	75.20
31-May	Total		80.00	14.00	

Debit the SALES RETURNS A/C   Debit the VAT a/c

Credit note total credited to CUSTOMER A/C

B ⟶

A: document totals are posted to the sales ledger – this shows how much each customer (debtor) owes us
B: day book totals are posted to the general ledger – this shows total sales, returns and VAT

Figure 16 Posting day books to the ledger – sales and sales returns

Purchases Day Book

Date	Details	Invoice No	Total (excl VAT) £	VAT £	Total (incl VAT) £
09-May	Wilson Bros	W967	280.00	49.00	329.00
12-May	KGB	997	180.00	31.50	211.50
24-May	Ahmed Ltd	AL34	60.00	10.50	70.50
31-May	Total		520.00	91.00	

Debit the PURCHASES A/C   Debit the VAT A/C   Credit SUPPLIER A/C with invoice total

Returns Outwards (Purchases Returns) Day Book

Date	Details	Credit Note No	Total (excl VAT) £	VAT £	Total (incl VAT) £
18-May	KGB	C05	8.00	1.40	9.40
29-May	Ahmed Ltd	CA12	32.00	5.60	37.60
31-May	Total		40.00	7.00	

Credit the PURCHASE RETURNS A/C   Credit the VAT A/C   Debit SUPPLIER A/C with credit note total

Purchases Ledger (Customer accounts)

Wilson Bros
| | 9 May Purchases 329.00 |

KGB
| 18 May Purchase returns 9.40 | 12 May Purchases 211.50 |

Ahmed Ltd
| 29 May Purchase returns 37.60 | 24 May Purchases 70.50 |

A →

General Ledger

Purchases
| 31 May Purchases DB 520.00 | |

Purchase returns
| | 31 May Purchases returns DB 40.00 |

VAT
| 31 May Sales returns DB 14.00 | 31 May Sales DB 147.00 |
| 31 May Purchases DB 91.00 | 31 May Purchases returns DB 7.00 |

B →

A: document totals are posted to the purchases ledger – this shows how much we owe each supplier (creditor)
B: day book totals are posted to the general ledger – this shows total purchases, returns and VAT

Figure 17 Posting day books to the ledger – purchases and purchase returns

CTIVITY

The solution to the activity on page 11, Guy Roper (Camping Supplies),
appears below.

Sales Day Book

Date	Details	Invoice No	Total (excl VAT)	VAT	Total (incl VAT)
			£	£	£
03-March	Hiking & Biking	1322	400.00	70.00	470.00
08-March	Windjammer Ltd	1323	800.00	140.00	940.00
09-March	Gales & Co	1324	80.00	14.00	94.00
23-March	Arctic Bedrolls	1325	2,400.00	420.00	2,820.00
31-March	Total		3,680.00	644.00	

Sales Returns (Day Book)

Date	Details	Invoice No	Total (excl VAT)	VAT	Total (incl VAT)
			£	£	£
14-March	Windjammer Ltd	C345	40.00	7.00	47.00
27-March	Arctic Bedrolls	C346	200.00	35.00	235.00
31-March	Total		240.00	42.00	

Purchases Day Book

Date	Details	Invoice No	Total (excl VAT)	VAT	Total (incl VAT)
			£	£	£
05-March	Mistral	453	600.00	105.00	705.00
15-March	Top Tents	214	1,200.00	210.00	1,410.00
21-March	Hardy Ridgepole	789	1,560.00	273.00	1,833.00
31-March	Total		3,360.00	588.00	

Purchase Returns Day Book

Date	Details	Invoice No	Total (excl VAT)	VAT	Total (incl VAT)
			£	£	£
12-March	Mistral	CN56	120.00	21.00	141.00
30-March	Hardy Ridgepole	C223	240.00	42.00	282.00
31-March	Total		360.00	63.00	

Figure 18

Task

Your task is to post the day book details to the ledger.
Before you begin rule up the following:
a) Sales ledger accounts – an account for each customer.
b) Purchase ledger accounts – an account for each supplier.
c) General ledger accounts for: sales, sales returns, purchases, purchase returns and VAT.

World Cups – book-keeping to trial balance

In the previous sections we have traced the transactions of a small business called World Cups for the month of May, its first month of trading.
The relevant explanations are on:
- pages 9–11 – recording credit sales, credit purchases, sales returns and purchase returns by listing original documents in the day books
- pages 22–24 – transferring the day book details to the ledger
- pages 14–17 – recording receipts and payments for the month into the ledger by double entry between the cash book and other relevant accounts.

All of the transactions for World Cups are shown in the Appendix (see pages 93–98).

The two-column cash book

This section explains how the cash book uses separate columns for bank and cash transactions.

The cashier will record receipts and payments in the cash book. Usually these involve the bank account, but some businesses also hold cash.

The two-column cash book has columns for:
- the bank account – to record money deposited, withdrawn and held in the business bank account
- the cash account – used where the business holds notes and coins on the premises and uses these when making payments.

> **Note!**
>
> So far we have assumed that the cash book records only banking transactions. In practice, a business may also keep cash on the premises.

Table 8 An example of two-column cash book entries

		Bank or cash a/c	Cash book entry
1 January	Opened a business bank account and deposited opening capital of £2,000	Bank	Debit
5 January	Bought a van for £500 paying by cheque	Bank	Credit

Cont'd

		Bank or cash a/c	Cash book entry
10 January	Withdrew £350 from the bank for use as office cash (NB this affects both cash and bank)	Bank Cash	Credit Debit
12 January	Bought stock for £200 paying in cash (purchases)	Cash	Credit
18 January	Sold stock for £500 cash (sales)	Cash	Debit
19 January	Paid £300 cash for rent	Cash	Credit
20 January	Sold stock for £400, received a cheque (sales)	Bank	Debit
25 January	Bought stationery for office use paying by cheque £100	Bank	Credit
28 January	Paid J Jones, a creditor, £150 by cheque	Bank	Credit

Table 9 *The cash book*

Debit							Credit	
Date	Details	Cash £	Bank £	Date	Details	Cash £	Bank £	
1 Jan	Capital		2,000	5 Jan	Van		500	
10 Jan	Bank C	350		10 Jan	Cash C		350	
18 Jan	Sales	500		12 Jan	Purchases	200		
20 Jan	Sales		400	19 Jan	Rent	300		
				25 Jan	Stationery		100	
				28 Jan	J Jones		150	
				31 Jan	Balances c/d	350	1,300	
		850	2,400			850	2,400	
1 Feb	Balances b/d	350	1,300					

Notice that:
- the bank account and the cash accounts are balanced separately
- the entry on 10 January appears twice on opposite sides of the book – this is called a **contra entry** (indicated by a 'C'). The complete double entry takes place within the book – between the bank and cash accounts.

Key term

Contra entry: Where money is transferred between the bank and cash accounts, two entries are required in the cash book: one bank entry and one cash entry. These are on opposite sides of the book – contra means opposite.

Tasks

1   In the example on page 27, the bank and cash accounts have debit balances on 1 February. What do these balances tell us? (Answer in one sentence.)
2   Recalculate the bank balance with the van bought on 5 January costing £2,500.
3   The bank should now have a credit balance – what does this tell us?
4   Why is a credit balance on the cash account impossible?
5   The payments on 12 and 28 January are both for stock purchased. Why are the details different – 12 January purchases a/c, 28 January Jones (the creditor) a/c? (Hint: think about the different conditions of payment in each case.)

Recording receipts from debtors and payments to creditors

The following example illustrates how receipts from debtors and payments to creditors are recorded in the cashbook together with double entries to the sales and purchases ledger.

The relevant accounts are shown below. Transactions for the first week in June are:

1 June   World Cups has a (debit) balance of £8,300 in the bank account
2 June   Received a cheque for £169.20 from JJ Ltd in full settlement of their account
3 June   Received a cheque for £20 from Patel & Co in part payment of their account
3 June   Withdrew £500 for use as office cash
4 June   Sent a cheque to Wilson Bros for £300 in part settlement of their account
5 June   Sent a cheque to KGB for £202.10 to settle their account
5 June   Balanced all of the above accounts.

The double entries in the ledger are shown in Figure 19 below:

Cash Book							
Dr							Cr
Date	Details	Cash	Bank	Date	Details	Cash	Bank
		£	£			£	£
1 June	Balance b/d		8,300.00	4 June	Cash C		500.00
2 June	JJ Ltd		169.20	3 June	Wilson Bros		300.00
3 June	Bank C	500.00		5 June	KGB		202.10
3 June	Patel & Co		20.00	5 June	Balance c/d	500.00	7,487.10
		500.00	8,489.20			500.00	8,489.20
6 June	Balance b/d	500.00	7,487.10				

Cont'd

Sales Ledger

Dr			JJ Ltd			Cr
Date	Details	£	Date	Details		£
1 June	Balance b/d	169.20	2 June	Bank		169.20

Dr			Patel & Co			Cr
Date	Details	£	Date	Details		£
1 June	Balance b/d	28.20	3 June	Bank		20.00
			5 June	Balance c/d		8.20
		28.20				28.20
6 June	Balance b/d	8.20				

Purchases Ledger

Dr			Wilson Bros			Cr
Date	Details	£	Date	Details		£
4 June	Bank	300.00	1 June	Balance c/d		329.00
5 June	Balance c/d	29.00				
		329.00				329.00
			6 June	Balance b/d		29.00

Dr			KGB			Cr
Date	Details	£	Date	Details		£
5 June	Bank	202.10	1 June	Balance c/d		202.10

> **Note!**
>
> Notice that where accounts have been settled in full there is no balance to bring down (because nothing is owed).

Figure 19 Ledger double entries

ACTIVITY

Double entry review questions

To answer questions 1–9 tick the appropriate box. In each case there is only ONE correct answer

1 An account which receives is: **a)** debited ☐

                                      b) credited ☐

2 How would you classify each of these accounts?

	Real a/c	Personal a/c	Nominal a/c
a) Bank	☐	☐	☐
b) Wages	☐	☐	☐
c) B Winston	☐	☐	☐
d) Machinery	☐	☐	☐
e) Insurance	☐	☐	☐
f) ABC Ltd	☐	☐	☐

29

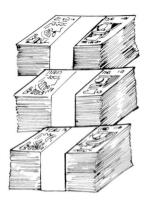

Money, money, money…

3 You set up in business by putting £2,000 of your savings into the business bank account. Which is the correct double entry?

   a) Debit bank a/c   Credit capital a/c   ☐

   b) Debit capital a/c   Credit bank a/c   ☐

4 The purchases a/c is debited:

   a) whenever we buy anything for the business   ☐

   b) only when we buy stock for resale   ☐

5 You buy a new delivery van for your business, paying by cheque. Which entry is correct?

   a) Debit bank   Credit purchases   ☐

   b) Debit purchases   Credit bank a/c   ☐

   c) Debit bank   Credit vehicles   ☐

   d) Debit vehicles   Credit bank   ☐

6 The sales account is always credited:

   a) True   ☐

   b) False   ☐

7 The trial balance is a list of the credit balances and a list of the debit balances on the books. It is used to:

   a) check that the double entries in the ledger are accurate   ☐

   b) find business profits   ☐

8 The business accounts are known as:

   a) 'T' accounts   ☐

   b) ledger accounts   ☐

   c) both   ☐

9 A real account shows:

   a) an asset   ☐

   b) a liability   ☐

   c) an expense   ☐

10 Opposite is your business bank account for the month:

   a) complete the double entries in the ledger accounts shown opposite.

   b) balance the bank account at 10 September.

   c) bring down the balance on 11 September.

   d) draw up a trial balance to check the ledger.

Bank

Date	Details	£	Date	Details	£
1 September	Capital	5,000	4 September	Equipment	1,000
7 September	Sales	2,200	5 September	Purchases	2,500
8 September	Sales	1,500	9 September	Rent	800

Capital

Date	Details	£	Date	Details	£

Equipment

Date	Details	£	Date	Details	£

Purchases

Date	Details	£	Date	Details	£

Sales

Date	Details	£	Date	Details	£

Rent

Date	Details	£	Date	Details	£

Trial balance

	Debit	Credit
	£	£
Bank		
Capital		
Equipment		
Purchases		
Sales		
Rent		

Summary

We have seen that:

- business transactions are recorded in the ledger accounts by means of double-entry book-keeping
- credit purchases, credit sales and returns are originally recorded in the day books. They are transferred to the ledger through:
  a) an individual entry in the personal account of the debtor (in the sales ledger) or creditor (in the purchases ledger), showing what is owed
  b) a monthly total entry to the purchases, sales, returns and VAT accounts (in the general ledger)
- receipts and payments are recorded in the cash book with a double entry to the ledger account which gave or received the money
- the accounts are balanced to find the state of each
- a trial balance is drawn up to check the accuracy of the ledger.

The activity below provides an opportunity to assess all of these processes.

 CTIVITY

Book-keeping to final accounts

 Deadly Lampshades is owned by Bella Donna, a sole trader, who sells antique-style lamps and light fittings. The business began trading on 1 January 200- and the first financial year will end on 31 December 200-, in one month's time. The books have been written up to the 30 November with balances brought down on 1 December.

Task 1

Begin by drawing up:

- Day books for: purchases, purchases returns, sales and sales returns
- Sales ledger accounts with balances brought down on 1 December:

Lumiere & Son	no balance
King Bros	no balance
Stadium Lights	£14,000 balance

- Purchases ledger accounts with balances brought down on 1 December:

B & G Supplies	£7,000 balance
Netcom Ltd	no balance

- Nominal ledger accounts with balances brought down on 1 December:

Wages and salaries	£4,762
Motor expenses	£5,890
Advertising	£6,700
Telephone	£3,566
Rent and rates	£8,450
Light and heat	£4,322
General expenses	£5,620

Stationery	£2,452
Purchases	£95,430
Sales	£182,560
Sales returns	£1,232
Purchases returns	£345
Furniture and fittings	£32,600
Vehicles	£24,230
Equipment	£26,000
Capital	£50,000
Bank loan	£20,000
Drawings	£22,500
Bank	£2,151

The transactions for December (the final month of the financial year) are shown below.

Notice that: all sales and purchases are on credit and all receipts and payments pass through the bank.

(For the purposes of this exercise ignore VAT except where stated.)

Date

1 Dec Paid motor repairs £520 by cheque

1 Dec Credit sales:

£1,200 + £210 VAT to Lumiere & Son (invoice 2000)

£2,000 + £350 VAT to King Bros (invoice 2001)

2 Dec Paid wages £45 by cheque

3 Dec Paid for stationery £35 by cheque

5 Dec Received a cheque for £2,400 from Stadium Lights

6 Dec Goods returned to us by King Bros £200 + £35 VAT (credit note C45)

7 Dec Bought new office chairs for £250 paid by cheque

9 Dec Paid electricity bill of £350 by cheque

10 Dec Credit sales:

£2,200 + £385 VAT to King Bros (invoice 2002)

£1,400 + £245 VAT to Stadium Lights (invoice 2003)

11 Dec Paid B & G Supplies £3,500 by cheque

12 Dec Paid business rates of £1,000 by cheque

14 Dec Credit purchases:

B & G Supplies £720 + £126 VAT (invoice B/6520)

Netcom Ltd £4,000 + £700 VAT (invoice 7878)

14 Dec Paid salaries £2,500 by cheque

15 Dec Returned damaged goods to Netcom Ltd £640 + £112 VAT (credit note 881)

17 Dec Wrote a cheque for £45 to pay for petrol

18 Dec Credit purchases:

£1,800 + £315 VAT from Netcom Ltd (invoice 8222)

19 Dec Returned goods to B & G Supplies £520 + £91 VAT (credit note BC/200)

19 Dec Goods returned to us by Stadium Lights £360 + £63 VAT (credit note C46)

23 Dec Paid £855 for advertising by cheque

24 Dec Lumiere & Son settled their account by cheque

25 Dec Closed until new year

Other information (needed for Task 3):
- Opening stock zero – this is the first year of trading
- Closing stock at 31 December = £15,320.

Task 2

1 Enter the transactions for December into the appropriate books.
2 At 31 December:
   - total all daybooks and transfer the totals to sales, purchases, returns and VAT accounts as appropriate
   - balance all ledger accounts.
3 Draw up a trial balance as at 31 December.
4 Write a brief note to explain the purpose of the trial balance. Explain, giving examples relating to the case study, its limitations as a means of checking the ledger.

Task 3

When you are familiar with final accounts complete the following task. Draw up the final accounts thus:
- trading and profit & loss account for year ending 31 December 200-
- balance sheet as at 31 December 200-.

Note: the business name will appear as Bella Donna trading as Deadly Lampshades.

Preparing financial statements – the final accounts

The business ledger accounts are a record of day-to-day transactions. A business will use this information to produce financial statements known as the final accounts. In the following sections we will look at the final accounts produced by: sole traders, partnerships, limited companies and non profit-making concerns.

The financial year

Each business works to a financial year: a 12-month period usually determined by the month in which the business began trading. For example the financial year of Pizza Express is 1 July to 30 June, whilst that of Manchester United is 1 August to 31 July.

The final accounts

At the end of each financial year a business is required, by law, to draw up a set of 'final accounts' for the benefit of its stakeholders. These consist of:

- the trading account
- the profit & loss account } these are drawn up together
- the balance sheet.

The final accounts must always be made available to the Inland Revenue for tax purposes; whether they are also made available to other stakeholders depends upon the type of organisation.

The trading period or accounting period

The period over which the final accounts report is called the trading (or accounting) period. This is never longer than a year but it may be less because:

- managers may wish to check performance more regularly e.g. weekly or monthly
- plcs (public limited companies) must produce interim final accounts every six months to satisfy the requirements of the London Stock Exchange.

Note!

Figure 1 on page 3 shows where the final accounts fit into the accounting process. Notice that they are prepared to inform the stakeholders (owners, investors, customers, suppliers, the government and the community) who have an interest in the business.

Drawing up the final accounts

The final accounts are the final stage in the accounting process. The procedure is as follows:

- the ledger accounts are balanced and a trial balance is extracted to check that the ledger is accurate
- the business carries out stock-taking to find the value of closing stock (unsold stock)
- the final accounts are drawn up from the figures on the trial balance as in the following table.

 Trial balances, pages 20–21

Table 10 *A trial balance*

Debit	Credit	
Expenses/costs incurred in purchasing stock	Sales revenue earned by selling stock	→ Trading account
Expenses/costs incurred in running the business (overheads)	Any other income such as: rents received, commission received	→ Profit & loss account
Assets (owned by the business)	Liabilities (borrowings from external sources)	
Drawings and other dividends (paid to the owner/s)	Capital (invested by the owners, i.e. sole traders, partners or shareholders)	→ Balance sheet

Note!

Each item on the trial balance appears once on the final accounts, either on the trading and profit & loss account or on the balance sheet.

Final accounts of a sole trader

Al Fresco has just completed his latest financial year. His book-keeper has drawn up a trial balance and prepared his final accounts (see Figure 24):

> Closing stock, the unsold stock at the end of the year, is valued by stock-taking (a physical check of remaining stock) at the end of the trading period. It is shown as additional information alongside the trial balance because it is needed to produce accurate final accounts. Unlike the trial balance items, it appears on both the trading account and the balance sheet.

Trial balance of Al Fresco as at 31 December 200-

	Debit £	Credit £	
Sales		180,000	Trading income (t)
Stock at 1 January 200-	17,500		Trading expenses (t)
Purchases	110,000		
Insurance	8,675		
Advertising	6,765		
Wages	17,500		Overhead expenses (p & l)
Light and heat	10,000		
General expenses	2,660		
Premises	150,000		Fixed assets (b)
Vehicles	4,800		
Debtors	18,000		Current assets (b)
Bank	5,700		
Creditors		12,000	Current liability (b)
Mortgage		48,000	Long-term liability (b)
Capital		140,000	Opening capital (b)
Drawings	28,400		Drawn by owner (b)
	380,000	380,000	

Additional information at 31 December 200-:
closing stock £12,000.

Trading adjustment (t)
Current asset (b)

Key: t = trading account, p/l = profit & loss account, b = balance sheet

Key terms

Closing stock is an 'adjustment' to the trial balance.
Opening stock, which is shown on the trial balance, is the closing stock from the previous period. A new business will have no opening stock in year one.

Figure 20

 Adjustments, page 42

> **Note!**
> The final accounts are drawn up in the vertical, or columnar, format. The left-hand column shows workings; the right-hand column shows the main totals.
>   The columns do not represent debits and credits.

The trading and profit & loss accounts are usually drawn up together. The heading includes the words 'year ending …' or 'period ending …'; the date is the last day of the trading period for which profits are being reported.

The trading account

The trading account calculates the gross profit achieved by buying and selling stock. It is used by traders such as wholesalers and retailers; service providers such as solicitors and accountants will not need a trading account.

Trading and profit & loss account of Al Fresco for period ending 31 December 200-

		£	£	
	Sales		180,000	The **trading account** shows **gross profit** (sales less cost of stock sold)
	Opening stock	17,500		
add	Purchases	110,000		
		127,500		
less	Closing stock	12,000		
	Cost of stock sold		115,500	
	Gross profit		64,500	
	Insurance	8,675		The **profit & loss account** shows **net profit** (or loss) (gross profit less total overhead costs)
	Advertising	6,765		
	Wages	17,500		
	Light and heat	10,000		
	General expenses	2,660		
			45,600	
	Net profit		18,900	

Note!

Remember that purchases only include stock bought for resale.

Figure 21

Notice that in the trading and profit & loss account the closing stock and net profit are highlighted. These are the only items that appear on both the trading/profit & loss account and the balance sheet.

Balance sheet of Al Fresco as at 31 December 200-

		£	£	
	Fixed assets			
	Premises		150,000	**net assets** (assets less liabilities)
	Vehicles		4,800	
			154,800	
	Current assets			
	Stock	12,000		
	Debtors	18,000		
	Bank	5,700		
		35,700		
less	**Current liabilities**			
	Creditors	12,000		
	Working capital		23,700	
			178,500	
less	**Long-term liabilities**			
	Mortgage		48,000	
	Net assets		130,500	equals
	As financed by:			
	Capital (at start)		140,000	**capital** (the value, or worth, of the business to the owner)
	Net profit		18,900	
			158,900	
	Drawings		28,400	
			130,500	

Note!

The bottom line on the balance sheet, the closing capital, represents the value of the business at the balance sheet date, i.e. what the owner should receive if it were sold.

Figure 22

The profit and loss account

The profit and loss account calculates **net profit** over the trading period by subtracting business overhead expenses from gross profit.

Overhead expenses are the business expenses consumed (used up) in the period. They do not include:

- fixed assets – which remain of value and appear on the balance sheet
- drawings – which are personal expenses of the owner rather than business expenses.

Businesses not using a trading account subtract running costs from sales.

The balance sheet

The bottom line shows the **worth** (or value) of the business. The words 'as at …' in the heading indicate that a balance sheet is a 'snapshot' of the business at a point in time.

The balance sheet must balance, i.e. **net assets** (assets less liabilities) = **capital** (capital at start + net profit – drawings). On Al Fresco's balance sheet these totals both equal £130,500. Each is double-underlined for emphasis.

As explained earlier, assets are resources owned by the business:

- **fixed assets** – are of long-term benefit to the business. Examples include: land, premises, plant, machinery, equipment, fixtures and fittings, vehicles
- **current assets** – are liable to change within the short term and probably from day to day. Examples are: (closing) stock, debtors, bank and cash balances, amounts prepaid (paid this period in advance for next period).

Liabilities, as indicated earlier, represent debts owed to external parties:

- **long-term liabilities** are amounts falling due after more than one year, such as bank loans and mortgages (possibly 25 years)
- **current liabilities** are amounts falling due within one year. They include: bank overdrafts (repayable on demand), trade creditors (usually payable in 30 days) and other short-term debts such as expenses due.

Working capital (or net current assets)

Working capital = current assets – current liabilities
(quickly turned (need to be paid in the near
into cash) future)

Working capital represents money available to run the business from day to day. A shortage – a cashflow problem – may cause a business to fail.

Working capital should not be confused with **capital**, which represents the funds invested by the owner. It is increased by **net profit** and reduced by **net loss**. It is also reduced by **drawings** (money or stock taken out of the business for the owner's personal use).

Key terms

Net profit is the value of sales less the value used up in making these sales.
Profit is value but not cash. Notice that net profit (the bottom line) is double-underlined.

Key term

The order of permanence – assets are listed on the balance sheet with, as far as possible, the longest lasting (most permanent) first: land and buildings before vehicles, etc.

Key terms

Working capital means the money available to run the business from day to day. This should not be confused with **capital**, which is money invested by the owner.

Note!

Note that negative figures are normally shown in brackets.

A net loss

It is unlikely that a business will make a gross loss – this would mean selling stock more cheaply than it was purchased. However, overhead costs may exceed gross profit so that net profit is negative, or a net loss. For example:

	Sales	180,000
less	Cost of stock sold	115,500
	Gross profit	64,500
less	Overheads	65,600
	Net loss	(1100)

A net loss is subtracted from capital on the balance sheet.

ASE STUDY

Worldcom or Worldcon?

In June 2002 the US company Worldcom was found to have misled investors through inaccuracies in its final accounts.

The case is complex, but essentially the company had treated some revenue expenses as if they were capital items. The effect was to increase profits (because less costs were shown) and to show a higher balance sheet value (because more fixed assets were shown).

The company did this in order to hide its financial difficulties and to reassure its investors. The US authorities took legal action against the company, which was found to have a 'black hole' in its accounts – millions of dollars were not accounted for.

CTIVITY

Tasks

1 If a company such as Worldcom fails, how are various stakeholders likely to be affected?
2 If Al Fresco treated his vehicles as a revenue expense what would be the effect on his accounts? Why would this matter?
3 Using the trial balance of Rip Van Winkle in the margin, draw up the final accounts on 30 June 200-.

Other items on the trading and profit & loss accounts

Carriage

Carriage is a delivery cost. **Carriage inwards** is the delivery cost of goods that we have bought. There may be carriage inwards on purchases and on fixed assets.

Capital versus revenue

Capital expenditure is expenditure on fixed assets. These will benefit the business over the long term and so must not be charged as an expense on the profit & loss account. They appear on the balance sheet.

Revenue expenditure is on day-to-day business expenses. They give only temporary benefit to the business and so can be written off as expenses to the trading and profit & loss account for the year in which they are consumed (used up).

Buying a car is a capital expense (it lasts a number of years).

Petrol and insurance are revenue (they are used up within the year).

Rip Van Winkle specialises in bedroom furniture. His latest figures are shown below:

Trial balance of Rip Van Winkle as at 30 June 200-

	Debit £	Credit £
Sales		261,320
Opening stock	7,650	
Purchases	152,630	
Motor expenses	1,537	
General repairs	4,000	
Wages and salaries	30,600	
Interest charges	280	
Rates and insurance	3,530	
Heating and lighting	3,656	
General expenses	2,353	
Drawings	21,000	
Land and buildings	125,000	
Fixtures and fittings	5,000	
Vehicles	7,200	
Debtors	3,114	
Creditors		6,680
Bank	450	
Bank loan		40,000
Opening capital		60,000
	368,000	368,000

Additional information available at the period end:
closing stock is valued at £9,540.

Some suppliers charge carriage on their invoices, others give free delivery, whilst some include carriage in the cost of goods. In order to be consistent we add carriage inwards to the cost of the item being delivered.

Carriage outwards is the cost of delivering goods to our customers. It is a distribution cost. Carriage outwards is charged as an expense on the profit & loss account.

Returns of stock

Purchase returns (returns outwards) occur when goods we have purchased are returned to our supplier. These goods should no longer be included as purchases. On the trading account we subtract purchase returns from purchases to show the net (real) purchases figure.

Sales returns (returns inwards) occur when goods we have sold are returned by our customers. These goods should no longer be included as sales. On the trading account we subtract sales returns from sales to show the net sales figure.

Discounts allowed and received

A business selling on credit may encourage customers to pay on time by offering a cash discount for prompt settlement of debts.

Discounts allowed are debts that we agree not to collect. They are a loss to our business and are charged as an expense on the profit & loss account.

Discounts received are a gain; our creditors will accept less than we were originally charged. They are added to gross profit on the profit & loss account.

Other items received

Sometimes income is generated apart from sales. Such items are identified by the word 'received'. They include rents received and commissions received. They too are added to gross profit on the profit & loss account.

Notice, in the example below, that a third column is needed for purchase returns.

Trading and profit & loss account of L Driver for period ending 28 February 200-

		£	£	£	
	Sales			9,300	
less	Sales returns			300	
				9,000	◀ ·········· Net sales
	Opening stock		1,200		
	Purchases	5,500			
less	Purchase returns	200			
			5,300		◀ ······ Net purchases
	Carriage inwards		500		
			7,000		◀ ·········· Purchases
less	Closing stock		1,000		including
	Cost of stock sold			6,000	carriage
	Gross profit			3,000	

Cont'd

add	Discounts received		500	◄······ Items received
	Rent received		700	
	Commission received		800	
			5,000	
less	Rent & rates	1,000		
	Discounts allowed	300		
	Carriage out	900		
	General expenses	800		
			3,000	
	Net profit		2,000	*Figure 23*

Ⓐ CTIVITY

1 Maurice Oxford, a motor mechanic, has just calculated his net profit for the year as £22,000. Unfortunately he has just realised that he has forgotten to include:

- returns inwards of £2,500
- carriage outwards of £850
- discounts received of £1,820.

Calculate what his net profit would be after taking these into consideration.

2 Janine Le Havre is the proprietor of Le Cafe Bleu. The book-keeper has just prepared the trial balance for the six months to 31 December 200-

Trial balance of Le Cafe Bleu as at 31 December 200-

Sales	75,000
Purchases	30,000
Carriage in	500
Returns in	860
Returns out	720
Discount received	520
Discount allowed	240
Stock	3,500
Salaries	25,000
Electricity and gas	2,000
Rent and rates	1,500
Carriage out	400
Premises	42,000
Equipment	10,000
Vehicles	4,500
Debtors	2,800
Cash at bank	4,350
Cash in hand	350
Creditors	3,760
Capital	55,000
Drawings	12,000
Bank loan	5,000

In addition: closing stock is valued at £3,000
a) Draw up a trial balance.
b) Prepare the trading and profit & loss accounts for the period ending 31 December 200-
c) Prepare the balance sheet as at this date.

Adjustments to the trial balance

The final accounts are drawn up using the ledger balances listed on the trial balance. However, in order to show a true profit and business value we may also need to take other relevant information into account and make some adjustments to the trial balance figures.

Adjustments may be needed for:
- closing stock
- accruals and prepayments
- provision for depreciation
- provision for bad debts.

Adjustments are normally listed as additional information below the trial balance. They must be shown on both the trading and profit & loss account and the balance sheet. Refer back to Al Fresco's final accounts on pages 36–37.

Notice that:
- the trial balance figures appear on **either** the trading and profit & loss account **or** the balance sheet – but not both
- the closing stock, an adjustment, which is not on the trial balance, appears on **both** the trading and profit & loss account **and** the balance sheet.

> **Key term**
>
> A **provision** is an estimated allowance.

 Provisions for depreciation, pages 46–52

 Provisions for bad debts, pages 53–55

Adjustment for closing stock

Procedure:
- On the trading account closing stock is subtracted from purchases. It remains of value and so should not be charged to this year. It reduces the cost of stock sold and so increases profit
- On the balance sheet closing stock is a current asset because it remains of value to the business.

> **Key term**
>
> **Closing stock** is the value of the stock that remains unsold at the year end.

Ⓐ CTIVITY

The final accounts of Al Fresco show a:
- closing stock of £12,000
- net profit of £18,900
- business value of £130,500 (balance sheet bottom line).

Tasks

1 What would be the profit and business value if:
   a) closing stock was not included?
   b) closing stock was valued at £20,000?
2 Are the following statements **true** or **false**?
   a) The higher the closing stock the higher the profit.
   b) The higher the closing stock the higher the value of the business.

Note!

From your answers you will see that the value of closing stock is important. The higher the closing stock, the higher the profit; the higher the business value, the lower the closing stock; and the lower the profit, the lower the business value.

The concept of prudence (see page 83) states that we must always show profit at its lowest. This is why stock must be valued at cost or current market value, whichever is lower.

Adjustments for accruals and prepayments

Remember that the trial balance figure shows the expenses we have paid in the trading period. It is unlikely that what we have paid will coincide with what we have used: some bills will be owing, some (such as insurance) may be paid ahead.

Accruals

The accruals concept says that on profit & loss we should charge for what we have used so we may need to make adjustments.

Procedure:
- On the profit & loss account add the accrual (the amount still due) to the trial balance figure
- On the balance sheet include the accrual as a current liability because it needs to be paid in the short term.

Prepayments

Procedure:
- On the profit & loss account subtract the prepayment from the trial balance figure
- On the balance sheet a prepayment is a current asset because it remains of value to the business at the period end.

For example, when we set out the final accounts of Al Fresco (on pages 36–37) we adjusted for closing stock. Suppose, however, that we now discover that some accruals and prepayments should also have been included.

Key term

Accruals are expenses due (or owing).

 Accruals concept, see page 83

Key term

Prepayments are expenses paid in advance.

Trial balance of Al Fresco as at 31 December 200-

	Debit £	Credit £
Sales		180,000
Stock at 1 January 200-	17,500	
Purchases	110,000	
Insurance	8,675	
Advertising	6,765	
Wages	17,500	
Light and heat	10,000	
General expenses	2,660	
Premises	150,000	
Vehicles	4,800	
Debtors	18,000	
Bank	5,700	
Creditors		12,000
Mortgage		48,000
Capital		140,000
Drawings	28,400	
	380,000	380,000

Additional information (adjustments) at 31 December 200-:
- Closing stock £12,000
- Insurance prepaid £675
- Wages due £1,500
- Light and heat due £350.

The accounts would now appear as follows. The adjustments are shaded for emphasis.

Trading and profit & loss account of Al Fresco for period ending 31 December 200-

		£	£
	Sales		180,000
	Opening stock	17,500	
add	Purchases	110,000	
		127,500	
less	Closing stock	12,000	
	Cost of stock sold		115,500
	Gross profit		64,500
	Insurance 8,675 – 675	8,000	
	Advertising	6,765	
	Wages 17,500 + 1,500	19,000	
	Light and heat 10,000 + 350	10,350	
	General expenses	2,660	
			46,775
	Net profit		17,725

Figure 24

Figure 25

Balance sheet of Al Fresco as at 31 December 200-

		£		£
	Fixed assets			
	Premises			150,000
	Vehicles			4,800
				154,800
	Current assets			
	Stock	12,000		
	Debtors	18,000		
	Bank	5,700		
	Prepayments	675		
		36,375		
less	**Current liabilities**			
	Creditors	12,000		
	Accruals	1,850		
		13,850		
	Working capital			22,525
				177,325
less	**Long-term liabilities**			
	Mortgage			48,000
	Net assets			129,325
	As financed by:			
	Capital (at start)			140,000
	Net profit			17,725
				157,725
	Drawings			28,400
				129,325

Figure 26

Check the accounts above with the original version on pages 36–37.

ACTIVITY

Check the accounts above with the original version on pages 36–37.

Task 1

What difference have the accruals and prepayments made to:
- the net profit?
- the business value (balance sheet total)?

Task 2

Use the following information to prepare:
- trading, profit & loss account for the period ending 30 June 200-
- balance sheet as at 30 June 200-.

Trial balance of Ron Bacardi as at 30 June 200-

	Debit £	Credit £
Sales		261,320
Opening stock	7,650	
Purchases	152,630	
Motor expenses	1,537	
General repairs	4,000	
Wages and salaries	30,600	
Interest charges	280	
Rates and insurance	3,530	
Heating and lighting	3,656	
General expenses	2,353	
Drawings	21,000	
Land and buildings	125,000	
Fixtures and fittings	5,000	
Vehicles	7,200	
Debtors	3,114	
Creditors		6,680
Bank	450	
Bank loan		40,000
Opening capital		60,000
	368,000	368,000

Additional information available at the period end:
- Closing stock is valued at £9,540
- General repairs of £150 are still due
- Wages and salaries due are £400
- Rates and insurance prepaid are £530.

Figure 27

Provision for depreciation

Why do we depreciate fixed assets?

Fixed assets are not written off as expenses in the profit & loss account in the year of purchase. They are capital expenses and are likely to remain valuable to the business for a number of years. However, these assets are unlikely to last forever. They will:
- wear out through use
- decay as a result of age
- become obsolete through changes in fashion or technology.

This loss must be recognised in the business books otherwise the final accounts will not give a true and fair view of the business finances.

CASE STUDY

House prices – a case in point

The rise in house prices since the 1970s has been dramatic. In 2002 the average London house was valued at £200,000.

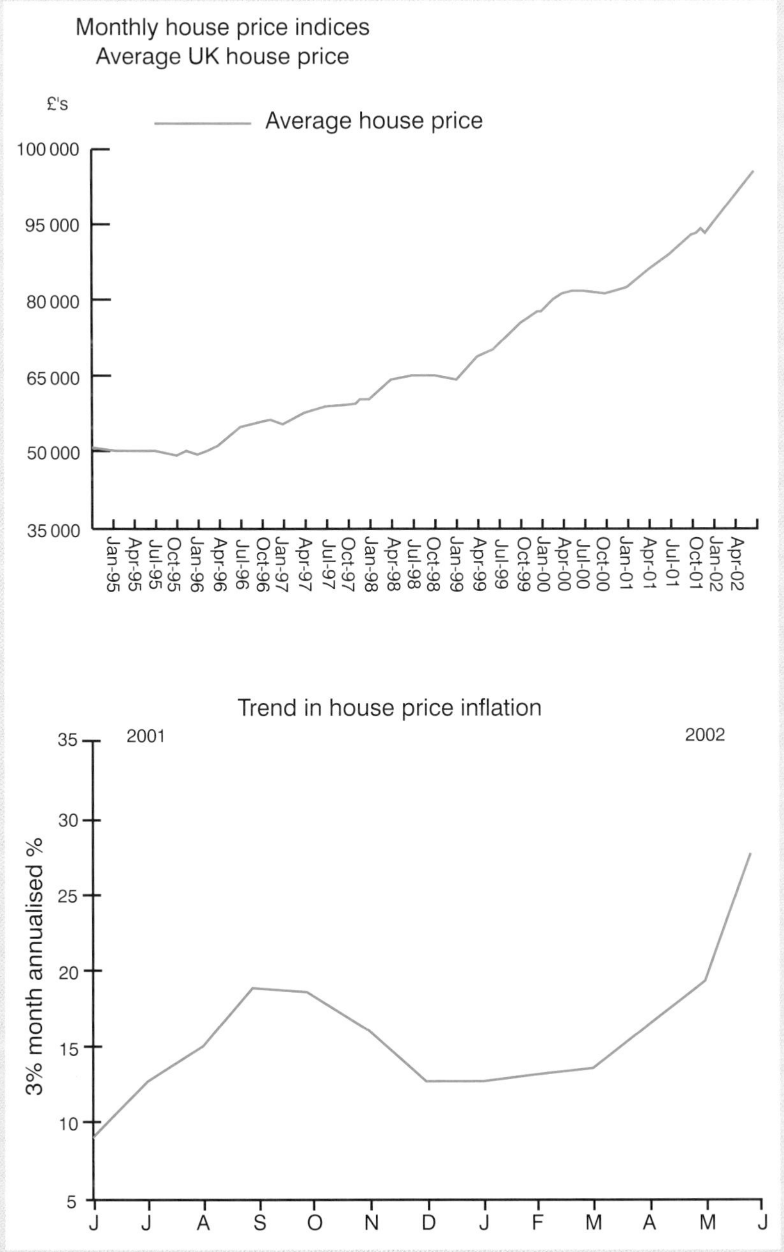

Monthly house price indices
Average UK house price

£'s

——— Average house price

Figure 29 House prices

Figure 28 *Inspector Morse's Jaguar, which sold for £85,000*

Trend in house price inflation

2001   2002

3% month annualised %

Accounting policies of
Tesco Plc, page 79

'Prudence' is one of the
favourite words of Gordon
Brown, who became Chancellor
of the Exchequer under the
new Labour Government.
Ironically, it means being
conservative (with a small 'c'),
i.e. being careful not to spend
money we do not have and not
anticipating profits before they
are made.

The concept of prudence
requires accountants, where
there is a choice, to show
profits and business value at
their lowest.

They should therefore make
provisions for (allow for):

- **depreciation on fixed
  assets**
- **doubtful debts, i.e.
  customers not paying
  what they owe.**

*Figure 30 Gordon Brown –
Chancellor of the Exchequer*

Activity

1 Complete the table using the list of assets below:

Useful life of asset	Company	Asset
40 years	My Travel Plc	?
20 years	My Travel Plc	?
10 years	Thistle Hotels Plc	?
5 years	Thistle Hotels Plc	?
3 years	Manchester United Plc	?

Assets: Aircraft, computers and software, property, motor vehicles,
furniture and fittings.

(Source: Annual reports)

2 What effect do you think that providing for depreciaiton will have on:
- business profits?
- business value?

What effect will appreciation have?

3 Land is likely to last indefinitely. Can you think of any circumstances in
which it may depreciate?

Why must we show depreciation in the final accounts?

The prudence concept states that where there is any doubt we must
show profits and business value at their lowest. Therefore, if we suspect
that our fixed assets are wearing out, we must allow for this in the
accounts, otherwise:
- profits will be overstated
- fixed asset value (and therefore the value of the business) will be
  overstated (and prudence will be offended).

How do we calculate depreciation?

The actual amount of depreciation charged is an estimate based upon
assumptions about the useful life of an asset.

Method 1: Straight-line method (also called the **equal instalment
method**)

This is the simplest and most popular method. Here depreciation on an
asset is the same amount each year. The calculation is:

$$\text{Annual depreciation} = \frac{\text{estimated loss in value over the life of the asset}}{\text{estimated life of asset (in years)}}$$

For example:

A machine costs £1,000 when new and will last for five years, after
which it will be worthless.

Annual depreciation $= \dfrac{£1,000}{5 \text{ years}} = £200$ p.a.

Sometimes a percentage figure is given instead of a number of years. For example, five years could be expressed instead as 20% per year (⅕ is 20%). In this case the formula becomes:

Depreciation p.a. $= \dfrac{\text{cost of asset} \times \% \text{ depreciation}}{£1,000 \times 20\%} = £200$ p.a.

Method 2: Reducing balance method (or the **diminishing balance** method)

Here an asset is depreciated by the same percentage each year. This is then applied to the asset value at the start of each year.

For example:
A machine costs £1,000 when new. It is to be depreciated at 20% p.a. on the reducing balance method:

		£
Year 1	Asset at cost	1,000
	less depreciation @ 20%	200
Year 2	Balance at start	800
	less depreciation @ 20%	160
Year 3	Balance at start	640
	less depreciation @ 20%	128
Year 4	Balance at start	512, etc. …

Each year the depreciation cost is lower, because the value of the asset is reducing over time. This may be more realistic for some assets.

> Residual or scrap value may need to be taken into account in the straight-line method. In the example, the asset loses all of its value over its life, but this does not always happen. For example, if the machine has an estimated scrap value of £200 its loss in value would be £1,000 – £200 = £800. Therefore:
> Annual depreciation $= \dfrac{(£1,000 - £200)}{5} = £160$ p.a.

 **CTIVITY**

Tasks

1 Calculate the annual depreciation for Archie Duke for years 1 and 2:

Asset	Cost	Depreciation method
Computers	£8,000	Straight-line method at 25% p.a.
Vehicles	£10,000	Reducing balance method at 25% p.a.

2 Calculate the annual straight-line depreciation on the fixed assets of Café Ole:

Asset	Cost	Estimated life	Residual value
Equipment	£10,000	4 years	zero
Vehicles	£4,500	5 years	£500

Depreciation and the trial balance

In recording depreciation we use two accounts for each asset:

- the asset account – this has a debit balance showing the asset at cost. This is unchanged by depreciation since cost is a historical fact
- a provision for depreciation account – this has a credit balance showing the depreciation to date. The balance grows as each year's annual depreciation is added.

Straight-line depreciation is worked out using cost so only the asset account is needed.

Reducing balance depreciation requires the value of the asset at the start of the year. This is found by comparing the two accounts of the trial balance thus:

Cost of asset – depreciation to date = asset value at start of year.

The accounts of Cindy Crayford below illustrate both methods.

Trial balance of Cindy Crayford as at 30 June 200-

	£	£
Sales		40,000
Purchases	22,500	
Salaries	14,000	
Electricity and gas	2,100	
Rent and rates	2,300	
Equipment (at cost)	9,000	
Provision for depreciation of equipment		900
Vehicles (at cost)	5,550	
Debtors	1,240	
Bank (overdraft)		500
Cash	50	
Creditors		1,840
Capital		20,000
Drawings	10,000	
Bank loan		3,500
	66,740	66,740

Details of depreciation appear below the trial balance. Cindy calculates depreciation thus:

equipment
10% reducing balance method
= 10% x (cost – depreciation to date)
= 10% x (£9,000–£900)
= £810

vehicles
20% straight-line method
= 20% x cost
= 20% x £5,550
= £1,110

Closing stock is valued at £3,000.
Depreciation is to be:
■ equipment 10% reducing balance method
■ vehicles 20% straight-line method.

Figure 31

Trading and profit & loss account of Cindy Crayford for year ending 30 June 200-

	£	£
Sales		40,000
Opening stock	0	
Purchases	22,500	
	22,500	
Closing stock	3,000	
Cost of stock sold		19,500
Gross profit		20,500
Salaries	14,000	
Electricity and gas	2,100	
Rent and rates	2,300	
Depreciation on equipment	810	
Depreciation on vehicles	1,110	
		20,320
Net profit		180

Profit & loss account

Depreciation for the year appears as an **expense**.
   The effect is to **reduce net profit**.

Figure 32

Balance sheet of Cindy Crayford as at 30th June 200-

	£ Cost	£ Dep to date	£ Net
Fixed assets			
Equipment	9,000	1,710	7,290
Vehicles	5,550	1,110	4,440
			11,730
Current assets			
Stock		3,000	
Debtors		1,240	
Cash		50	
		4,290	
Current liabilities			
Creditors		1,840	
Bank O/D		500	
		2,340	
Working capital			1,950
			13,680
Long-term liabilities			
Bank loan			3,500
			10,180
Capital			20,000
Net profit			180
			20,180
Drawings			10,000
			10,180

Balance sheet

Depreciation to date is calculated as follows:

Equipment
£810 this year + £900 in previous years (see trial balance) = £1,710

Vehicles
£1,110 this year + nothing in previous years (see trial balance) = £1,110

The asset **net value** is calculated as:
asset cost less depreciation to date.

Figure 33

The concept of consistency

There is a choice of depreciation methods: straight-line and reducing balance. In each case accountants must choose the most appropriate method and use this consistently from year to year. To swap from year to year would affect the business results and make comparisons difficult.

How do we show depreciation in the final accounts each year?

Depreciation is shown in final accounts as follows:

- depreciation for the period is charged as an expense to the profit & loss account – this reduces net profit
- total depreciation to date (provision at start + this year's depreciation) is deducted from the cost of the asset on the balance sheet.

ACTIVITY

Task 1

Look at the examples of Cindy Crayford's accounts (pages 50 and 51).

1 What would have been Cindy's net profit if depreciation were not shown?
2 What would be the value of each fixed asset if depreciation were not shown?
3 Which fixed assets of a business (any business) are unlikely to depreciate?

Task 2

Use the year end figures for Southwark Supplies to draw up the trading and profit & loss account and balance sheet at the end of year.

Trial balance of Southwark Supplies as at 31 December 200-

	£	£
Sales		414,250
Opening stock	70,000	
Purchases	275,500	
Heating and lighting	14,750	
Salaries	36,600	
Post and packaging	1,400	
Insurance	3,800	
Advertising	3,400	
Premises	120,000	
Fixtures and fittings (at cost)	45,000	
Provision for depreciation		
– fixtures and fittings		9,000
Debtors	55,000	
Bank	9,000	
Creditors		47,000
Opening capital		195,000
Mortgage		4,200
Drawings	35,000	
	669,450	669,450

Figure 34

Year end adjustments:
- Closing stock £60,000
- Salaries £400 prepaid
- Insurance £250 prepaid
- Heating and lighting £350 due
- Advertising £765 due
- Annual depreciation to be provided:
  fixtures and fittings 10% straight-line method.

Bad debts

Bad debts occur when a debt cannot be collected. This may happen because of:
- bankruptcy – a debtor goes out of business and has no money
- death – a debtor dies leaving insufficient funds
- dishonesty – a debtor gives false details or disappears leaving no forwarding address.

Ledger entries for bad debts

When a bad debt is discovered:
- the debt is removed from the debtor account (as it is no longer an asset)
- it is transferred to the bad debts account (a business expense).

Example:

On 31 August we learn that one of our customers, Four Star Hotels Ltd, has gone bankrupt, owing us £1,000. We write off the debt as follows:

> **Note!**
>
> If a limited company goes bankrupt there is a risk that some of its suppliers will not be paid. Remember that limited liability protects the private funds of company shareholders from creditors.

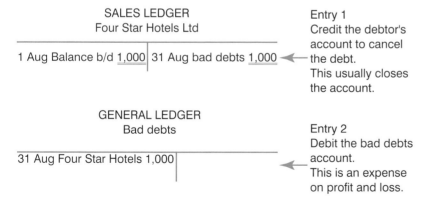

SALES LEDGER
Four Star Hotels Ltd

1 Aug Balance b/d 1,000 | 31 Aug bad debts 1,000

Entry 1
Credit the debtor's account to cancel the debt.
This usually closes the account.

GENERAL LEDGER
Bad debts

31 Aug Four Star Hotels 1,000

Entry 2
Debit the bad debts account.
This is an expense on profit and loss.

Figure 35 An example of a bad debt

The trial balance

Writing off bad debts has two effects:
- the trial balance shows bad debts as a debit alongside other expenses

- the total debtors will have been reduced by the amount of the bad debt.

Final accounts

If bad debts have already been written off, i.e. if they appear on the trial balance then:

- bad debts appear as an expense on the profit & loss account
- the debtors figure (already reduced remember) appears as a current asset in the usual way.

The final accounts of Flying Saucers (Greek cuisine) opposite give an example of provision for bad debts.

Provision for bad or doubtful debts

Why do we make a provision for bad or doubtful debts?

Even after we have written off known bad debts, we may still suspect that some of our remaining debtors will not pay – even though we have no particular debtor in mind. Perhaps we know from experience that 'someone always lets us down' or maybe current trading conditions are difficult so it is likely that some of our customers will struggle.

Whatever the reason, if we suspect that some of our debts cannot be collected then we must adjust our debtors figure accordingly; we cannot leave an asset on the balance sheet if we do not believe it to be accurate.

How do we estimate the provision for bad (or doubtful) debts?

The estimate for bad (or doubtful) debts is usually based upon past experience and is normally expressed as a percentage of existing debtors.

For example, if debtors on the books owe £3,000, and we suspect that 10% are doubtful then the provision for the year is:
£3,000 × 10% = £300.

Provision for bad (or doubtful) debts on the trial balance

This year's provision, like all adjustments, will appear below the trial balance. Last year's provision (if any) will appear as a credit balance on the trial balance.

The difference between these two figures, i.e. any increase or decrease, is needed in making the entries to the final accounts.

Provisions for bad (or doubtful) debts in the final accounts

Entries to the profit & loss account show the difference between this year's and last year's provision. Possibilities are an increase, a decrease or no change.

 Prudence, page 83

> When a business fails the assets are sold and the creditors paid.
>
> If the business is insolvent, i.e. if there are insufficient assets to pay the creditors in full, then:
>
> - creditors' claims are put in order – the government will be at the top and the owners at the bottom (this is the risk of being in business)
>
> - sole traders and partners may have to pay off outstanding debts from their own personal assets or out of future earnings, whereas the shareholders of limited companies will not. Limited companies must clearly display the abbreviations Ltd or plc in their names so that their creditors know of the risk they take in trading with them.
>
> The protection afforded by limited liability partly explains why companies are subject to more accounting regulations than other businesses.

Final accounts of Flying Saucers (Greek cuisine)
Trial balance as at 31 May 200-

	Debit	Credit
	£	£
Opening stock	2,550	
Purchases	23,880	
Sales		95,200
Administration	17,370	
Salaries	55,000	
Bad debts (written off)	1,200	
Provision for bad debts		150
Furniture and fittings	34,000	
Equipment	18,000	
Debtors	5,000	
Bank (overdrawn)		2,415
Creditors		4,235
Capital		60,000
Drawings	5,000	
	162,000	162,000

Closing stock £3,400
Provision for bad debts 5%
i.e. £5,000 x 5% = £250

Trading and profit & loss account
for the period ending 31 May 200-

		£		£
Sales				95,200
Opening stock		2,550		
Purchases		23,880		
		26,430		
Closing stock		3,400		
Cost of stock sold				23,030
Gross profit				72,170
Bad debts		1,200		
Bad debts provision – increase		100		
Administration		17,370		
Salaries		55,000		
				73,670
Net loss				(1,500)

Balance sheet as at 31 May 200-

		£		£
Fixed assets				
Furniture and Fittings				34,000
Equipment				18,000
				52,000
Current assets				
Stock		3,400		
less Debtors (£5,000 – £250)		4,750		
		8,150		
Current liabilities				
Creditors		4,235		
less Bank (overdrawn)		2,415		
		6,650		
				1,500
				53,500
Financed by				
Capital				60,000
Net loss				(1,500)
				58,500
Drawings				5,000
				53,500

Figure 36 Final accounts and trading and
profit & loss account of Flying Saucers

55

Table 11 *Provision for bad or doubtful debts*

Final account	If increase in provision	If decrease in provision	If no change in provision
Profit & loss account	Enter the 'increase in bad debts' as an expense Note: If there was no previous provision then the whole provision is an expense	Enter the 'decrease in bad debts' as a gain – this is added to gross profit	No entry is needed
Balance sheet	Subtract the whole of this year's provision from debtors – this shows a true and fair value for existing debtors		

CTIVITY

Sole trader final accounts

Rena Shah is a sole trader who trades as Towerview.

Rena has produced the following ledger balances at the end of her most recent financial year:

Account balances as at 31 October 200-

	£
Sales	202,000
Sales returns	1,500
Stock at start	16,000
Purchases	140,000
Purchase returns	1,200
Carriage in	2,500
Rates	3,400
Heat and light	3,800
Repairs	1,420
Bad debts	200
Insurance	1,800
Advertising	950
Telephone	860
Vehicles	3,500
Interest charges	1,450
Vehicle expenses	3,640
Sundry expenses	2,270
Premises	78,000
Fixtures and fittings	5,000
Debtors	6,200
Bank	1,450

Creditors	8,300
Capital (at start)	32,440
Mortgage	48,000
Drawings	18,000

Additional information:
- Closing stock £17,560
- Motor repair bill due £245
- Business rates prepaid £1,000

Provision for depreciation to be:
- Vehicles 8% straight-line
- Fixtures and fittings 6% straight-line

Provision for bad debts:
- 5% on remaining debtors.

Tasks

1 Draw up a trial balance.
2 Draw up the final accounts at 31 October 200- to comprise:
   - trading and profit & loss account
   - balance sheet.
3 Explain what the final accounts show and why they are prepared annually.
4 Explain and illustrate how the following accounting conventions affect the preparation of these accounts:
   - prudence
   - accruals
   - consistency.

The final accounts of partnerships

What is a partnership?

A partnership is an association of people carrying on in business together with a view to making a profit.

In general there may be between two and 20 partners, although some professional organisations such as accountants and solicitors are allowed to exceed this number.

The fact that the business has a number of owners, all of whom are entitled to share in the profits (and bear the losses) of the business, means that it is sensible to make an agreement about such matters.

The Partnership Act (1890)
The act states that where no partnership agreement is made then:
- profits & losses must be shared equally between partners
- no partner is entitled to a salary
- partners are not entitled to interest on capital
- interest is not to be charged on drawings
- if more capital than agreed is invested then 5% interest p.a. should be paid on the excess.

Companies House, page 68

The partnership agreement (or deed)

Partners will usually draw up a partnership agreement (or deed) to set out the rules under which the business is to be run. This normally covers matters such as salaries, interest, drawings, share of profits, etc. Where the partners do not make a partnership agreement such matters are covered by the Partnership Act.

Liability for debts and Limited Liability Partnerships (LLPs)

Normally all partners are personally liable for business debts and liability is unlimited. However, the Limited Liability Partnership Act 2000 now makes it possible for any new or existing firm to gain limited liability. The reasoning is that larger partnerships may need the protection of limited liability in modern trading conditions. It is believed that many thousands of partnerships will become LLPs, but at the time of writing few have done so.

LLPs share profits as a partnership but have to disclose information in a similar way to a limited company. This means they must file their accounts at Companies House where they are available for inspection by interested parties.

The final accounts of partnerships

The final accounts of a partnership are similar to those of a sole trader. Differences only arise where it is necessary to take into account that there is more than one owner. This affects the way that profits (or losses) are shared and the way that capital is shown.

The differences are:
- an appropriation account is drawn up as a final section at the end of the profit & loss account. This shows how profits are to be divided between partners
- a capital account for each partner is shown on the balance sheet. Unlike a sole trader's capital this is not affected by profits or drawings but is 'fixed' at the original capital invested. It will change only if a partner invests new capital or reduces capital
- a current account for each partner is shown on the balance sheet. This shows each partner's opening balance, adds to this the profits to which the partner is entitled and subtracts any interest on drawings owed and drawings taken. A positive balance indicates that profits are still available to the partner, a negative balance indicates that profits have been overdrawn.

Red and Blue Travel Company

Red and Blue run an Australian travel firm. Their accounts are shown over the next few pages.

Trial balance of Red and Blue as at 31 January 200-

	£	£
Fixtures and fittings	10,500	
Equipment	16,000	
Sales		50,000
Opening stock	3,000	
Purchases	30,000	
Rent and rates	3,400	
Heat and light	2,000	
Insurance	2,100	
General expenses	2,500	
General administration	1,000	
Debtors	2,400	
Bank	3,100	
Creditors		2,500
Bank loan		8,000
Red – Capital account		12,000
Current account		1,000
Drawings	3,000	
Blue – Capital account		8,000
Current account	500	
Drawings	2,000	
	81,500	81,500

Figure 37

Additional information:
- closing stock is valued at £4,000
- partners are charged interest on drawings at 5% p.a.
- Red and Blue are each entitled to a salary of £2,000 p.a.
- interest on capital of 10% is agreed
- remaining profit is shared as Red 3⁄5 and Blue 2⁄5

Adjustments are not shown in the examples, but these are all exactly the same as for a sole trader.

Trading and profit and loss account of Red and Blue for period ending 31 January 200-

		£	£	
	Sales		50,000	
	Opening stock	3,000		
	Purchases	30,000		
		33,000		
less	Closing stock	4,000		Trading and profit
less	Cost of stock sold		29,000	& loss account
	Gross profit		21,000	exactly as for a
				sole trader
less	Rent and rates	3,400		
	Heat and light	2,000		
	Insurance	2,100		
	General expenses	2,500		
	General administration	1,000		
			11,000	
	Net profit		10,000	
				Interest charged to
add	**Interest on drawings**			compensate partners
	Red 5%	150		who draw less than
	Blue 5%	100		others
			250	Sum to be shared
			10,250	
less	**Salaries**			
	Red	2,000		
	Blue	2,000		
			4,000	
			6,250	Shows how profits are
	Interest on capital			allocated to partners
	Red 10%	1,200		
	Blue 10%	800		
			2,000	
			4,250	
	Share of profits			
	Red $\frac{3}{5}$	2,550		
	Blue $\frac{2}{5}$	1,700		
			4,250	Shows that all profit
			0	has been shared

Figure 38

Balance Sheet of Red and Blue as at 31 January 200-

	£	£	£	
Fixed assets				
Fixtures and fittings		10,500		
Equipment		16,000		
		26,500		
Current assets				Assets and
Stock	4,000			liabilities exactly
Debtors	2,400			as for a sole
Bank	3,100			trader
	9,500			
less **Current liabilities**				
Creditors	2,500			
Working capital		7,000		
		33,500		
less **Long-term liabilities**				
Bank loan		8,000		
		25,500		

As financed by:	**Red**	**Blue**		
Capital accounts	12,000	8,000	20,000	Original capital invested
Current accounts				
Opening balances b/d	1,000	(500)		Current account at start
add Salary	2,000	2,000		Share of profit
Interest on capital	1,200	800		from appropriation
Share of profits	2,550	1,700		account
	6,750	4,000		
less Drawings	3,000	2,000		Drawings set off against profits
Interest on drawings	150	100		Owed to partners
	3,600	1,900	5,500	on current account
			25,500	Total owed to partners

Figure 39

Notice that:

- interest on drawings may be charged to compensate those partners who draw less than others
- fixed amounts such as salary and interest on capital must be appropriated first. The share of profits comes last and divides any remaining amount
- share of profits can be expressed as either: a fraction 3⁄5 and 2⁄5, a percentage 60% and 40%, or a ratio 3:2

- capital and current accounts normally have credit balances on the trial balance; if so they are positive figures on the balance sheet
- Blue has a debit current account balance at start indicating that in previous years profits have been overdrawn by £500. This appears as a negative figure on his current account and so is subtracted from this year's profit
- Red has a credit balance indicating that £1,000 of available profits have not yet been drawn. This appears as a positive figure on the current account and is added to this year's profits.

ACTIVITY

Trial balance of King & Singh as at 31 December 200-

		£	£
Capital accounts:	King		10,000
	Singh		6,000
Current accounts:	King		480
	Singh		380
Drawings:	King	2,400	
	Singh	1,400	
Purchases		15,260	
Sales			39,056
Stock at 1 Jan		3,560	
Debtors		7,860	
Creditors			3,820
Premises		50,000	
Equipment		1,320	
Provision for depreciation			
– equipment			264
Salaries		5,760	
Rent and rates		880	
General administration		840	
Mortgage			40,000
Bank		9,120	
Cash		1,600	
		100,000	100,000

Figure 40

Additional information at the year end:
- closing stock at 31 December 200- valued at £4,000
- administration expenses still due of £117
- rates prepaid of £80
- depreciation on equipment to be calculated on the straight-line method
- equipment life estimated at 10 years after which it will have no value.

The Partnership Deed shows that:
- partners will be charged 5% p.a. interest on drawings
- partners will be paid 7% interest p.a. on capital
- Singh will receive an annual salary of £4,000
- remaining profits/losses will be shared in a ratio of 2:1 between King and Singh respectively.

Tasks

Prepare a full set of final accounts for the partnership as follows:

1 The trading and profit & loss account for the year ending 31 December 200-, to include the appropriation of profits/losses by partners (to the nearest £1).

2 The balance sheet as at 31 December 200-, to include capital accounts and current accounts of partners.

The final accounts of clubs and societies

Clubs, societies and associations aim to provide a benefit for their members, rather than to make a profit. Examples include local sports clubs (e.g. tennis club, bowls club, cricket club, etc.).

Some clubs and societies are large scale, e.g. building societies, the RAC (Royal Automobile Club), and the AA (Automobile Association).

The difference between the accounts of profit-making organisations and clubs and societies

Although clubs, societies and associations are **not-for-profit**, the treasurer will still need to keep accounts. The fact that there is no profit motive means that there are some differences in the terms used.

Table 12 *Comparison of terminology*

Terms used by profit-making organisations	Equivalent terms used by clubs and societies
Capital	**Accumulated fund** (or **capital fund**): this shows the value of the organisation. It is used to provide a service for the members
Drawings	Members do not withdraw funds for personal use
Profit	**Surplus**: any surplus is ploughed back into the accumulated fund. It does not benefit members financially but enables the club to provide a better service
Loss	**Deficit**: deficits decrease accumulated fund

Table 13 *Comparison of account types*

Accounts used by profit-making organisations	Equivalent accounts used by clubs and societies
Cash book	**Receipts and payments account**: records receipts and payments
Trading account	**Trading account**: where clubs regularly trade they too may use a trading account. For example a social club may have a trading account showing bar sales, cost of sales and profit on the bar
Profit & loss account	**Income & expenditure account**: shows running costs (revenue expenses) and surplus or deficit
Balance sheet	**Balance sheet**: shows assets, liabilities and **accumulated fund**

The accounts supplied to the members usually consist of:

- a statement of affairs calculating the accumulated fund at the start of the year. This is a summarised opening balance sheet showing: **total assets – total liabilities = accumulated fund**
- an income and expenditure account (including a trading account if appropriate). This lists revenue income and expenditure and calculates surplus or deficit for the period
- a balance sheet showing assets, liabilities and accumulated fund.

Adjustments

Where necessary, figures are adjusted for provisions, accruals and prepayments in the usual way. However, the income and expenditure account can pose some problems:

- start of year accruals and prepayments must also be taken into account. This is not necessary with other forms of organisation because the trial balance figures include this information
- income, in particular subscriptions, can be accrued and prepaid. The sales of profit-making organisations never need to be adjusted because of the way they are recorded.

The treatment of adjustments is expenses (rent, electricity, etc.) and incomes (e.g. subscriptions).

Table 14 *Expenses*

	If accrued at start	If prepaid at start	If accrued at end	If prepaid at end
Entry on income and expenditure account for the year	Subtract from expense	Add to expense	Add to expense	Subtract from expense
Opening and closing balance sheet entries	Current liability (owed by us)	Current asset (value owed to us)	Current liability (owed by us)	Current asset (value owed to us)

Table 15 *Incomes*

	If accrued at start	If prepaid at start	If accrued at end	If prepaid at end
Entry on income and expenditure account	Subtract from income	Add to income	Add to income	Subtract from income
Opening and closing balance sheet entries	Current asset (owed to us)	Current liability (value owed by us)	Current asset (owed to us)	Current liability (value owed by us)

The Faldo-on-Sea Golf Club

Look at the accounts for the Faldo-on-Sea Golf Club on page 66. The club's treasurer has assembled the following information for the year ended 30 September 200-.

1 At 1 October 200- (the start of the year) the assets and liabilities of the club were:
   - fixtures and fittings costing £3,000, depreciation to date £300
   - equipment costing £2,000, depreciation to date £200
   - bank balance of £160, repair bill still due £60, rent prepaid £100
   - a long-term loan of £1,000.

The receipts and payments for the year are shown below:

Receipts and payments account (summary) for the year to 30 September 200-

Receipts	£	Payments	£
Bank balance b/d at		Bar expenses	2,850
1 Oct	80	Expenses for dinner	
Subscriptions	1,800	dance	1,000
Bar sales	6,000	Rent of clubhouse	850
Tickets for dinner dance	1,820	Repairs	515
Donations	600	Electricity and heating	450
		Groundsman's wages	1,220
		General expenses	65
		Golf equipment	500
		Bank balance c/d at 30	
		Sept	2,850
	10,300		10,300
Bank balance b/d at 1 Oct	2,850		

Figure 41

Remember that this is the club cash book.

2 At 30 September 200- (the year end) adjustments are to be made for:
   - insurance prepaid £20
   - electricity due £70
   - depreciation on existing fixed assets at 20% on cost (straight-line method).

This information is used to produce three year-end statements for the members:
   - a statement of affairs at start to show accumulated funds
   - the income and expenditure account to show surplus or deficit for the year
   - the balance sheet at the year end.

Statement of affairs as at 1 October 20-0

	£	£
Assets		
Fixtures and fittings		2,700
Equipment		1,800
Bank		160
Rent prepaid		100 a
		4,760
less **Liabilities**		
Repairs due	60	
Loan	1,000	
		1,060 b
Accumulated fund		3,700

Income and expenditure a/c for year ended 30 September 20-1

	£	£
Income		
Subscriptions		1,800
Profit on bar		3,150
Profit on annual dinner dance		820
Donations		600
		6,370
less **Expenditure**		
Rent of clubhouse (850+100)	950	a
Repairs (515–60)	455	b
Electricity and heating (450+70)	520	c
Groundsmans wages	1,220	
Insurance (65–20)	45	d
Depreciation – fixtures and fittings	300	
Depreciation – golf equipment	250	
		3,740
Surplus		2,630

Accruals and prepayments in income and expenditure account

At start of year:
a) £100 rent received last year but relating to this year – must be added in this year
b) £60 repairs due for last year but received this year – must be subtracted as they relate to last year

At year end:
c) £70 electricity due this year must be included
d) £20 insurance prepaid must be subtracted

Balance sheet as at 30 September 20-1

	£	£	£
	Cost	Dep-to-date	Net
Fixed assets			
Fixtures and fittings	3,000	600	2,400
Equipment	2,500	450	2,050
			4,450
Current assets			
Bank		2,930	
Insurance prepaid		20	d
		2,950	
less **Current liabilities**			
Electricity due		70	c
Working capital			2,880
			7,330
less **Long-term liabilities**			
Loan			1,000
			6,330
Represented by:			
Accumulated fund (at start)			3,700
add Surplus			2,630
			6,330

Figure 42 Accounts for the Faldo-on-Sea Golf Club

The final accounts of limited companies

Limited companies raise capital by selling shares. This gives them the potential to raise more funds than either sole traders or partnerships. Shareholders, who own the business, are rewarded by the payment of dividends (a share of annual profits). Shares can be resold to other investors for the market price.

Setting up a company (incorporation)

The main reasons for incorporation are:

- to raise more funds through the issue of shares
- to gain the security of limited liability. This protects the private funds of shareholders if a business fails. At most they will lose the share capital they have invested, or agreed to invest.

Types of company

- private limited companies may not offer their shares for sale on the Stock Exchange. These tend to be smaller, often family-owned companies. They may wish to restrict share ownership so as to keep control. They carry the word 'limited' (or Ltd) after the company name as a warning to creditors
- public limited companies sell their shares to the general public or other businesses via the Stock Exchange or other markets. These tend to be larger companies needing substantial amounts of capital. Shares are freely traded and, since the company cannot easily control who buys them, ownership of the company may change. Many companies, for example, become subsidiaries of other companies, i.e. they are owned and controlled by them. The abbreviation 'plc' appears after the company name.

The London Stock Market and plc shares

Shares of plcs are freely transferable, i.e. they can be bought and sold by members of the general public and by other businesses (known as institutional investors). This dealing takes place on the stock market where the price is set by supply and demand. There is:

- the primary market where companies raise funds by floating new issues of shares
- the secondary market where investors can trade 'second-hand' shares. This is the bulk of day-to-day trading.

Larger plcs have an official listing. The FTSE-100 measures prices of the top 100 of these. Smaller plcs appear on AIM – the alternative investment market.

> **Limited liability was introduced in the mid-nineteenth century at a time when companies needed to raise large sums of money for projects such as the building of the railways. Under existing law shareholders were liable for every penny their company owed and could be ruined if a project failed. Naturally, many were unwilling to invest. The protection of limited liability was introduced to encourage more investors to buy shares.**

> **When a company is set up two documents are needed:**
>
> - **the memorandum of association, which sets out the information needed by those outside of the company including the company name and address; the fact that it has limited liability; its objectives, and the authorised share capital**
>
> - **the articles of association, which set out the company's internal rules and regulations.**

London STOCK EXCHANGE

Regulation of accounts,
page 84

Company details and copies of their accounts are available at Companies House:

www.companies-house.gov.uk

The board of directors

The chairman runs meetings of the board of directors. The managing director (or chief executive in the USA) is responsible for day-to-day management of the company. Executive directors are employed by the company as top managers; non-executive directors are experts in certain areas. They are brought in from time to time to give advice. They have other jobs (perhaps as MPs) and may be non-executive directors of a number of businesses.

How are companies different from sole traders and partnerships?

Companies are different from sole traders and partnerships in a number of ways:

- sole traders and partners make business decisions and take the responsibility for these – a company, on the other hand, is a separate legal entit; the company itself can make contracts, sue and be sued and pays corporation tax on its profits
- there is a separation between the ownership and management of a company – the shareholders who own the company will appoint a board of directors to run the company on their behalf; the directors then have a duty of stewardship; they must use the shareholders' funds wisely and try to produce a reasonable financial return
- company shareholders have limited liability; unlike sole traders and partners they will never have to pay business debts from their own pockets.

Regulation of limited company accounts

Companies are subject to a higher degree of financial regulation than other business organisations:

- the Companies Acts of 1985 and 1989 require companies to keep accurate accounts and produce final accounts which show a 'true and fair view' of business performance
- the Accounting Standards Board draws up professional accounting standards which companies must follow
- plcs are also subject to the rules of the Stock Exchange.

Regulations are needed because the size of many companies means that their activities affect a large number of people. The idea is to make company directors more accountable to the external stakeholders including:

- the shareholders who own the company and have invested their money in it
- the creditors who, because of limited liability, might not be paid if the business fails
- the community as a whole.

The final accounts of a limited company comprise:

- a trading account (where appropriate)
- a profit & loss account – to include an appropriation account
- a balance sheet
- a cashflow statement (required for large companies only and not shown here).

The accounts are similar in many respects to those of sole traders and partnerships. Differences arise where it is necessary to take account of the different form of ownership, therefore:

- an appropriation account shows how profits are shared
- the capital section of the balance sheet shows shareholders' funds.

Channel Water Ltd

Look at the final accounts of Channel Water Ltd below, to page 73.

Channel Water Ltd trial balance as at 31 December 200-

	£	£
Land and buildings	550,000	
Equipment	115,000	
Vehicles	62,000	
Sales		1,800,000
Stock at 1 Jan	180,000	
Purchases	1,000,000	
Rent and rates	14,500	
Heat and light	4,500	
Advertising	3,200	
Salaries	202,400	
Directors' fees	73,600	
Insurance	6,000	
Interest charges	4,800	
General expenses	115,200	
Debtors	350,800	
Bank (overdraft)		19,000
Creditors		178,700
Debentures		96,000
Issued share capital		
6% preference shares – 50,000 of £1 each		50,000
Ordinary shares – 450,000 of £1 each		450,000
Capital reserves		
Revaluation reserve		50,000
Revenue reserves		
Profit & loss account balance		5,300
General reserve		33,000
	2,682,000	2,682,000

Figure 43

Additional information:

Closing stock at 31/12/01 was valued at £210,000.

The directors have recommended:

- to pay the full dividend on Preference shares of 6%
- to pay a dividend pence per share on Ordinary shares of 10p
- to provide for Corporation tax of £25,000
- to transfer to the General Reserve £15,000.

The trading and profit & loss accounts

These are similar to those for other organisations although:

- directors' salaries (or fees) are charged to profit & loss because company directors are employees
- debenture interest (like all finance and interest charges) is charged to profit & loss.

Trading and profit & loss account of Channel Water Ltd
for the period ending 31 December 200-

		£	£
	Sales		1,800,000
	Opening stock	180,000	
	Purchases	1,000,000	
		1,180,000	
less	Closing stock	210,000	
less	Cost of stock sold		970,000
	Gross profit		830,000
less	Rent and rates	14,500	
	Heat and light	4,500	
	Advertising	3,200	
	Salaries	202,400	
	Directors' fees	73,600	
	Insurance	6,000	
	Bad debts	0	
	Interest charges	4,800	
	General expenses	115,200	
			424,200
	Net profit		405,800
less	Corporation tax		25,000
	Profit attributable to shareholders		380,800
less	Proposed dividends:		
	% Preference dividend	3,000	
	Ordinary dividend per share	45,000	
			48,000
			332,800
less	Transfer to general reserve		15,000
			317,800
add	Profit & loss balance b/d		5,300
	Profit & loss balance c/d		323,100

Appropriation of account

– shows how profit is distributed

Figure 44

Balance sheet of Channel Water Ltd as at 31 December 200-

	£	£	
Fixed assets			
Land and buildings		550,000	
Equipment		115,000	
Vehicles		62,000	
		727,000	
Current assets			
Stock	210,000		
Debtors	350,800		
	560,800		
less **Current liabilities**			
Creditors	178,700		
Bank O/D	19,000		Proposed
Proposed dividend	48,000		◄····payments not
Corporation tax due	25,000		◄········yet made
	270,700		
Working capital		290,100	
		1,017,100	
less **Long-term liabilities**			
Debentures		96,000	
		921,100	
Financed by:			
Authorised share capital			
50,000 6% preference shares of £1 each		50,000	For information
500,000 ordinary shares of £1 each		500,000	only – not
		550,000	included in
			balance sheet
Issued share capital			totals
50,000 6% preference shares of £1 each		50,000	
450,000 ordinary shares of £1 each		450,000	
Capital reserves			
Share premium account		0	
Revaluation reserve		50,000	Balance from
			profit &
Revenue reserves			loss account
Profit & loss account		323,100	◄········
General reserve		48,000	◄········
			£33,000 balance
Shareholders' funds		921,100	(on trial balance)
			plus £15,000
			on appropriation
			account

Figure 45

The appropriation account

This follows the profit & loss account and shows the three uses of profit:

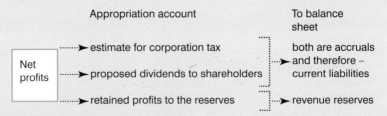

Figure 46 *The three uses of profit*

The balance sheet

The capital section of the balance sheet reflects company ownership by shareholders.

Authorised share capital (nominal capital) is the share capital that the company is allowed to issue. It is listed for information, but is not added into the totals. The registrar of companies must approve any new share capital.

- Preference shares pay a set rate of interest each year and carry less risk. They are paid ahead of ordinary shares when annual profits are shared and also when a business is being wound up. Most preference shares are cumulative so that interest not paid in one year can be made up in the next. They may be issued to family members, business founders or top directors
- Ordinary shares (also called equities or risk capital) form the majority of shares. The dividend, which is measured in pence per share, varies with profits. It is proposed by directors and must be approved by the shareholders at the AGM (annual general meeting).

Issued (or called up) share capital is the capital that the company has actually raised, i.e. the shares it has sold and been paid for. Sometimes shares are issued in stages or paid for in instalments. For these reasons issued capital may only be part of the authorised capital.

Market capitalisation is the total market value of a company's shares on the stock market. This is based upon what investors will pay for a share. It will vary from day to day and is often very different from the balance sheet value which is, broadly speaking, what the assets would fetch if the company were broken up and sold off.

In the 1990s, market prices became unrealistically high – market value was often far higher than balance sheet value. The fall in market prices since the millennium is a readjustment as prices drop to more realistic levels.

Companies raise funds when they sell new issues of shares, after that the shares can be resold as investors try to make a gain. Most of the trading on the stock markets concerns this selling of second-hand ordinary shares of plcs. It therefore raises no money at all for the companies involved. The market share price is, however, of interest to the companies because:

- **they may wish to sell new issues of shares in future and will want a high price**
- **a high share price keeps the investors happy. It shows confidence in the company and, presumably, that the directors are doing a good job**
- **a low share price makes the company cheap to buy. It could be taken over by another company.**

Reserves are additions to share capital. There are:
- revenue reserves – these are retained profits and include general reserves and profit & loss balance from the appropriation account
- capital reserves – these are gains not made through normal trading. They include:
  - revaluation reserve (an increase in asset value, such as property)
  - share premium account (where issued share capital exceeds authorised capital, the additional value raised is listed in the share premium account. This might occur when market demand is high so that new issues of shares may be sold at a premium, e.g. shares with a nominal [or face] value of £1 may sell for £1.20, representing a premium of 20p per share).

Corporation tax for the year appears as a current liability; it is an estimate that will not have been paid by the balance sheet date.

Dividends appear as current liabilities. They will have been proposed, but not yet paid, by the balance sheet date.

 **CTIVITY**

Final accounts of a limited company

Red Oak Ltd has just completed its latest financial year.

Trial balance as at 31 December 200-

	£	£
Land and buildings *at cost*	350,000	
Fixtures and fittings *at cost*	90,000	
Vehicles *at cost*	60,000	
Sales		2,355,450
Stock at 1 Jan	252,000	
Purchases	1,652,140	
Rent and rates	29,200	
Heat and light	14,500	
Advertising	23,260	
Salaries	242,100	
Directors' fees	173,200	
Provision for depreciation on fixtures and fittings		9,000
Insurance	23,000	
Interest charges	14,800	
General expenses	40,200	
Debtors	250,000	
Bank (overdraft)		18,950
Creditors		178,700

Debentures	96,000
Authorised and issued share capital:	
8% preference shares – 65,000 shares of £1 each	65,000
Ordinary shares – 450,000 shares of £1 each	450,000
Reserves:	
Profit & loss account balance	8,300
General reserve	33,000
3,214,400	3,214,400

Figure 47 *Trial balance for Red Oaks Ltd as at 31 December 200-*

Additional information at 31 December:
- Closing stock valued at 282,470
- General expenses due £4,500
- Interest charges due £500
- Insurance prepaid £1,200
- A provision for bad debts to be created of 2% of existing debtors
- Depreciation on vehicles p.a. to be 20% on the straight-line method
- Depreciation on fixtures and fittings is to be 10% on the reducing balance method.

In addition the directors have recommended:
- Payment of the full 8% dividend on preference shares
- A dividend of 10p per share on ordinary shares
- A provision for corporation tax of £40,000
- A transfer to the general reserve of £50,000.

Task

Your task is to set out the final accounts to include:
- the trading and profit & loss account (including an appropriation account) for the period ending 31 December 200-
- the balance sheet as at 31 December 200-.

Published accounts of limited companies

Disclosure of information to stakeholders

The law takes the view that a number of groups have a legitimate interest in the performance of a limited company. These stakeholders include:
- the shareholders who own the business. Although some shareholders are also directors, the majority take no part in running the companies. They must trust the directors to use their money wisely
- debenture holders who have leant money to the business

- creditors who are owed money. Remember that shareholders have limited liability so creditors are at risk of not being paid if the business fails
- employees – who are concerned about job security and pay. They may be interested to see how much directors are paid
- customers – who might wish to see lower prices or alternatively more investment in a more efficient or a safer service
- the community in general, which may be affected by the economic and environmental impacts of business decisions, for example the effects on employment, the atmosphere, the countryside, noise levels and so on. They may also have moral concerns about the treatment of animals, suppliers or communities in developing countries.

The case study of Railtrack shows that a variety of stakeholder groups need to see the annual reports. It also shows that these groups may be interested for very different reasons (see pages 5 and 6).

The Companies Acts of 1985 and 1989 – disclosure of information

The Companies Acts require limited companies to disclose a minimum amount of financial information to their stakeholders. The main requirements are that companies must:

- keep accurate accounting records of the company's transactions
- publish an annual report and accounts comprising: a profit & loss account, a balance sheet, a cashflow statement (for larger companies), an auditors' report and a directors' report
- present the report and accounts to the shareholders (or members) and debenture holders for approval at the annual general meeting (or AGM). Here the main events of the year will be highlighted and details such as the dividends the directors propose to pay to shareholders, the election of directors and the appointment of auditors will be discussed and voted on. The accounts must be accepted by the shareholders
- send a copy of the report and accounts to the registrar of Companies at Companies House. On payment of a small fee anyone may inspect these accounts which must disclose a minimum amount of information about the business
- the accounts should be audited (checked) by an independent auditor (although some smaller businesses are exempt from this). A firm of chartered accountants will be appointed by the shareholders for this purpose. The purpose of the audit report is to confirm that the accounts are a 'true and fair view'. It is read aloud at the annual general meeting.

Companies listed on the Stock Exchange must also:

- publish an interim report six months into the financial year
- disclose certain additional information about their activities including a geographic analysis of trading results.

CASE STUDY

A reputation in shreds

2002 was a disastrous year for Arthur Anderson, one of the world's largest auditors. The firm was auditor for the giant US company Enron which crashed with no warning. An investigation into why the auditors failed to spot a 'black hole' (missing cash) in the company's accounts discovered that vital documents had been shredded by the accounting firm.

Investors and business partners were among those who suffered. Employees lost not only their jobs but also their company pensions. There were calls for tougher accounting regulations to prevent similar frauds.

For some time it has been clear that auditors have found difficulty in spotting problems. For example, in the UK in the 1990s, Polly Peck failed despite being given a clean audit report. Terry Smith pointed out in his book *Where were the auditors?* that a number of problems were not being detected.

Task

What are the problems if an unsound company gets a clean audit report? (Think about why the companies acts require an independent audit.)

The published accounts consist of:
- a profit & loss account – including an appropriation section. There will also be a trading account if appropriate
- a balance sheet – signed by one director as evidence of company approval of the accounts
- a cashflow statement (required for larger companies)
- notes to the accounts
- accounting policies
- auditors' report – addressed to the members of the company
- directors' report.

The following are often also provided:
- chairperson's statement
- review of activities
- summary of results
- notice of AGM.

On pages 77–78 are extracts from the published accounts of Tesco PLC.

Terms used in the published accounts:
- **comparative figures**. The present year's figures are accompanied by figures from the previous year for purposes of comparison
- **group accounts**. Many companies are part of a group of companies controlled by a holding company, a plc which holds more than 50%

Table 16 Tesco PLC: group profit and loss account, 52 weeks ended 23 February 2002

	2002 £m	2001 £m	Notes
Turnover	23,653	20,988	Sales
Cost of sales	(21,866)	(19,400)	
Gross profit	1,787	1,588	
Administration expenses	465	422	Cost of sales and running costs
Operating profit	1,322	1,166	Net profit from normal trading operations
Share of operating profit on joint ventures	42	21	Profits from business which Tesco runs with other companies
Loss on disposal of assets	(10)	(8)	Some assets have been sold for less than book value
Profit on ordinary activities before interest and taxation	1,354	1,179	
Net interest payable	(153)	(125)	Interest on loans and bonds
Profit on ordinary activities before taxation	1,201	1,054	
Taxation	(371)	(333)	Corporation tax
Profit on ordinary activities after taxation	830	721	
Minority interests	–	1	Profits from business in which Tesco has a minority interest
Profit for the financial year	830	722	The profit 'attributable to shareholders' – i.e. this belongs to the shareholders
Dividends	(390)	(340)	The share of profit to be paid to shareholders
Retained profit	440	382	The remaining profit to be reinvested in the business. This appears in the reserves on the balance sheet
	Pence	Pence	
Earnings per share	12.05	10.63	(Profit attributable to shareholders less preference dividends)/the number of ordinary shares
Dividend per share	5.6	4.98	The dividend to be paid on each ordinary share

* Notice that in published accounts where expenses are to be subtracted they are shown as negatives

Table 17 Tesco PLC: group balance sheet as at 23 February 2002

	2002 £m	2001 £m	Notes
Fixed assets			
Intangible assets	154	154	Goodwill
Tangible assets	11,032	9,580	Land, buildings, plant, equipment, fixtures and fittings, motor vehicles
Investments	317	304	Investments in joint ventures
	11,503	10,038	
Current assets			
Stocks	929	838	Closing stocks of goods for resale
Debtors	454	322	Tesco stores sell on a cash basis, these are debtors from other companies in the group
Investments	225	255	Short-term deposits
Cash in bank and hand	445	279	
	2,053	1,694	
Creditors: falling (due within one year)	(4,809)	(4,389)	Loans, overdrafts, trade creditors (suppliers), accruals for taxation, dividends and operating expenses
Net current assets/(liabilities)	(2,756)	(2,695)	Working capital
Total assets – current liabilities	8,747	7,343	
Creditors: falling (due after more than one year)	(3,181)	(2,329)	Bank loans and bonds
Net assets	5,566	5,014	
Capital and reserves			
Called up share capital	350	347	5p ordinary shares. Authorised: 9,200 million shares issued: 6,994 million shares
Share premium account	2,004	1,870	Resulting from shares issued above face value
Other reserves	40	40	
Profit & loss account	3,136	2,721	Retained profits
Shareholders' funds	5,530	4,978	
Minority interests	36	36	
Total capital employed	5,566	5,014	

of its shares. The holding (or parent) company is required to publish consolidated accounts showing the position of the group as a whole. It may also publish a company account showing the parent company accounts only

Revenue reserves and capital reserves, pages 71–72

- **minority interests**. Group accounts include the profits of subsidiaries. However, these may not be wholly owned by the group. For example, a group may own 60% of the shares in a subsidiary. Those who own the remaining 40%, the minority interest, must be recognised as having a claim to profits
- **extraordinary items**. These occur outside the ordinary course of business and are not expected to recur. An example might be cost associated with making staff redundant after a business reorganisation
- **income from shares in participating interests**. This includes the group's share of profits and losses in related companies

Some alternative balance sheet terms are used in published accounts:

- **creditors amounts falling due within one year**. These are the current liabilities
- **creditors amounts falling due after more than one year**. These are long-term liabilities.

Below is an extract from the accounting policies of Tesco PLC:

Basis of preparation of financial statements

These financial statements have been prepared under the historical cost convention, in accordance with applicable accounting standards and the Companies Act 1985.

Basis of consolidation

The Group financial statements consist of the financial statements of the parent company, its subsidiary undertakings and the group's share of interests in joint ventures and associates.

Turnover

Turnover consists of sales through retail outlets and sales of development properties excluding value added tax.

Stocks

Stocks ... are valued at the lower of cost and net realisable value.

Money market deposits

Money market deposits are stated at cost. All income from these investments is included in the profit & loss account as interest receivable

Fixed assets and depreciation

Fixed assets are carried at cost.

Depreciation is provided on a straight-line basis over the anticipated useful economic lives of the assets. The following rates apply to the year ended 23 February 2002:

- Freehold buildings 2.5%
- Leasehold buildings by equal annual instalments over the remaining years of the lease
- Plant, equipment, fixtures and fittings and motor vehicles at rates varying from 10% to 33%.

Source: Tesco PLC Annual Report, February 2002

The auditors' report

The companies acts require that independent external auditors should inspect the accounts to see if they present a 'true and fair view' of the business' finances. The audit is carried out by a firm of chartered accountants appointed by the shareholders.

If the auditors are not satisfied they will raise concerns by presenting a 'qualified report'.

Below is a statement by the auditor of Tesco PLC.

Independent auditors' report to the members of Tesco PLC

We have audited the financial statements which comprise the profit & loss accounts, balance sheets ... which have been prepared under the historical cost convention and the accounting policies set out in the statement of accounting policies.

Our responsibility is to audit the financial statements in accordance with relevant legal and regulatory requirements ...

Respective responsibilities of directors and auditors

We report to you our opinion as to whether the financial statements give a true and fair view and are properly prepared in accordance with the Companies Act 1985. We also report to you if, in our opinion, the Directors' report is not consistent with the financial statements, if the company has not kept proper accounting records, if we have not received all the information and explanations we require for our audit, or if information specified by law ... is not disclosed.

Basis of opinion

We conducted our audit in accordance with auditing standards issued by the Auditing Practices Board. An audit includes ... an assessment of the significant estimates and judgements made by the Directors and of whether the accounting policies are appropriate to the company.

We planned and performed our audit so as to obtain ... sufficient evidence to give reasonable assurance that the financial statements are free from material misstatement, whether caused by fraud, or other irregularity or error.

Opinion

In our opinion the financial statements give a true and fair view of the state of affairs of the company and the Group at 23 February 2002 and of the profit and cash flows of the Group for the year then ended and have been properly prepared in accordance with the Companies Act 1985.

PriceWaterhouseCoopers, Chartered Accountants and Registered Auditors
London, 9 April 2002

Source: Tesco PLC Annual Report, February 2002

The accounts show that the auditors were paid £800,000 for their services.

The directors' report
The following should be included:
- the principal activities of the company
- a review of the business activities during the year, the position at the year end and an indication of future developments
- any important post balance sheet events
- proposed dividends and transfers to the reserves
- difference between book value and actual value of fixed assets
- company policy for the employment of disabled persons
- directors' names, shareholdings or debenture holdings in the company
- political or charitable contributions made by the company
- details of events affecting the company over the year
- research and development activities
- any buying back of the company's own shares
- how employees are informed of company activity
- creditor payment policy.

ACTIVITY

Task 1
Obtain copies of the annual report and accounts of three different plcs. To do this you might:
- telephone the company
- use the company website – a search engine will locate it for you
- use the *Financial Times* free annual report club. The details are available in the Companies and Markets section of the *Financial Times*.
- use either of the following websites:
    1   World Investor Link http://www.wilink.com/
    2   Carol http://www.carol.co.uk/
In our experience a printed copy is easier to use than hard copy from the company website.

   Locate each of the sections of the annual report mentioned above and note down the page numbers.

Task 2
Note down the following details:
1   from the profit & loss account – turnover, gross profit (if any), pre-tax profit/loss, provision for corporation tax, dividends proposed, retained profits, earnings per share
2   from the balance sheet – issued capital, shareholders' funds (the difference will be the reserves)

3 from the notes to the accounts – identify the accounting procedures used for: stock valuation and depreciation

4 from the auditors' report – whether the auditors found the accounts to be satisfactory.

Look up who the auditors were and how much they were paid.

(Where there is a choice use the group [or consolidated] accounts.)

Task 3

Read the present share price of the business in a newspaper or on its website. See if you can get a graph of the share price over the last year from the London Stock Exchange, http://www.londonstockexchange.com.

1 Does the directors' report help you explain the main price changes?

2 What is the market capitalisation and how does this compare with the balance sheet value?

Task 4

1 Who are the main shareholders?

2 How much are the directors paid?

3 How many shares do they hold?

4 What were these worth? (You will need the share price.)

Accounting concepts and the regulation of accounting

Financial accounting is concerned with classifying, measuring and recording the transactions of a business. It is also concerned with using the financial records to produce financial statements for the benefit of stakeholders.

A true and fair view

In order for reports such as the trading and profit & loss account and the balance sheet to be useful they must give the correct impression about business finances and they must be believed by the stakeholders who read them. The companies acts call this 'a true and fair view'. This can only be achieved if accounts are prepared to an agreed set of standards.

In the UK, business financial statements are prepared according to accounting concepts which have grown up over time.

Financial statements are regulated by:
- rules drawn up by the accounting profession – the SSAPs and FRS
- companies acts passed by parliament.

Accounting standards and laws are primarily designed to regulate the activities of limited companies and to inform and protect their stakeholders.

Sole traders and partnerships are subject to far less regulation. We discuss these separately below.

Accounting concepts

Over time a number of concepts have been adopted as accepted accounting practice. These include:

- **Going concern concept**
  In drawing up the accounts it is assumed that the business will continue to operate into the foreseeable future. No values in the accounts should indicate otherwise.
  The point here is that if a business is about to close then certain values will change. For example equipment, which is valuable to the business whilst it is operating, may be impossible to sell if the business closes.

- **Prudence concept** (formerly called **conservatism**)
  Where there is doubt, figures must be used which maximise costs and minimise expenditure. In other words, a business must always be pessimistic about its profits and value. As an example:
  stock is always valued at the lowest possible estimate, i.e. at either cost or present market value, whichever is the lower.
  Assets must be depreciated in an attempt to show their state of use; doubtful debts provision must be made if debtors are thought unlikely to pay.

- **Accruals concept** (also called the **matching concept**)
  Income and expenditure should be matched to the accounting period in which a sale is made or a cost incurred, rather than to the period in which money is received or paid. So for example when calculating profits:
  - prepayments for a future period are subtracted from this year's costs
  - accruals (payments still due for this year) are added to this year's costs.

- **Consistency**
  In some situations different accounting techniques are available. This concept requires accountants to choose the most appropriate technique and use this from year to year. So for example:
  - the depreciation method should always be either reducing balance method or straight-line method
  - stock valuation should always be either LIFO (last in first out), FIFO (first in first out) or AVCO (average cost).
  Constant changes will lead to changes in business results which have nothing to do with business performance. Of course a technique may be changed where there are good reasons – see FRS 18 (below).

- **Materiality**
  The accounts should only record details that are significant to the affairs of the business. It is a waste of time and effort to record trivial items or to go into unnecessary detail. For example:
  an electrical plug may last many years but is not recorded as a fixed

asset because it is not of sufficient value; recording the use of paperclips may be possible but not worthwhile.

Information about the plug and the paperclips will take time to record but will not significantly alter our view of business performance.

- **Separate valuation principle** (or **business entity concept**)
  The values in business accounts relate only to the business; the private assets and liabilities of the owners are a separate issue. Drawings, for example, are not shown as a business expense but are subtracted from owner's capital on the balance sheet. What the drawings are used for is nothing to do with the business. Sometimes with sole traders and partnerships there may be a sharing of assets and other facilities: a car may be used as 50% private use and 50% business use, the telephone bills may be split and so on. Such agreements are frequently accepted by the Inland Revenue as legitimate. However, the principle remains that the values in the business accounts relate only to the business.

- **Money measurement concept**
  The business accounts only show what can be measured in monetary terms and can therefore only give a partial picture of the business. The accounts do not show whether the management team is good or bad, whether the product range is about to become hopelessly out of date, whether a competitor is about to wipe them out, the morale of staff and so on.

  In recent years there have been attempts to encourage companies to undertake social reporting and green/environmental audits to give a fuller picture to stakeholders.

Regulation of the accounting process

A number of regulations exist to ensure that the accounts do indeed provide a true and fair view. Some are drawn up by the professional accounting bodies, others are statutory (legal) requirements. Regulation comes from:

- professional accounting standards issued by the Accounting Standards Board. These include: SSAPs (Statements of Standard Accounting Practice) and FRS (Financial Reporting Standards)
- the Companies Acts (1985 & 1989) drawn up by parliament
- requirements of the Stock Exchange (for listed plcs)
- international accounting standards drawn up by the European Union.

SSAPs (Statements of Standard Accounting Practice)

By the 1960s it was clear that different accountants were using very different methods when preparing accounts. As a result, 25 SSAPs were introduced between 1970 and 1990. The aim was to provide clear and detailed guidance on the preparation of accounting statements.

FRS (Financial Reporting Standards)

FRS were first introduced in 1990 to update the SSAPs, which they are gradually replacing. FRS18, for example, has superseded SSAP2, which formerly set standards for the disclosure of accounting policies.

FRS 18 accounting policies

This was introduced in June 2001 to update and replace SSAP2.
It states that accounting policies must comply with accounting standards and company legislation. The published accounts must disclose the accounting policies used and any changes made to these under FRS 18:

- the notes to the published accounts should confirm that the accounts have been prepared in accordance with accounting standards
- accounting policies should be reviewed regularly and changed if another policy is thought more likely to give a true and fair view
- each policy used must be: relevant, reliable, comparable and understandable and the cost of providing information should not outweigh the gain.

The Companies Acts (1985 & 1989)

These acts of parliament apply to limited companies only. They are the price that companies pay for the protection of limited liability and are designed primarily to:

- protect the shareholders by ensuring that the directors are fulfilling their duty of stewardship over the shareholders' capital, i.e. they are using it wisely and working to provide them with a reasonable return
- protect the creditors from limited liability, which could result in them not being paid.

The following sections are especially relevant:

- section 221, which is concerned with keeping full and accurate accounts
- section 222, which is concerned with the disclosure of accounting information to stakeholders.

Requirements of the Stock Exchange (for listed plcs)

As well as producing annual accounts listed companies must also provide an interim (half-yearly) set of accounts.

Listed companies have their shares traded on the main London Stock Market. The accounts must also include additional information such as a geographical breakdown of turnover (see extract opposite).

International accounting standards

Directives from the European Union have attempted to establish minimum accounting standards for member countries.
The Companies Act of 1989 amended the 1985 Companies Act to bring the treatment of group accounts and the regulation of auditors into line with European law.

Requirements of the Acts
page 75

Tesco: geographical analysis of turnover

The Group's operations of retailing and associated activities and property development are carried out in the UK, Republic of Ireland, France, Hungary, Poland, Czech Republic, Slovak Republic, Thailand, South Korea and Taiwan.

	Continuing operations	Turnover (excluding VAT)
	2002 £m	2001 £m
UK	20,052	18,372
Rest of Europe	2,203	1,756
Asia	1,398	860
Total	23,653	20,988

(Source: Tesco Annual Report, February 2002 – notes to financial statements, note 2)

The regulation of sole traders and partnerships

Unlike companies, the accounts of sole traders and partnerships (with the exception of Limited Liability Partnerships) are subject to very little regulation. This is because there is less risk from their actions to external stakeholders. These businesses are owned by the people who run them, and these owners are personally responsible for every penny of business debts.

Sole traders and partnerships must submit final accounts each year to the Inland Revenue for income tax purposes. Apart from this there are few formal requirements. The accounts do not have to be drawn up by an accountant or externally audited. However, they should be accurate and they should be prepared on an accruals basis so as to match revenues and expenses to the relevant year.

If annual turnover is below £15,000 a self assessment tax form should be completed to show totals for: turnover (sales), business expenses and annual profit but no final accounts are needed.

If turnover exceeds £15,000 then a profit & loss account and balance sheet must accompany the tax form.

Computerised accounting

The role of information technology in financial accounting

Many businesses, including small sole traders, now produce their financial statements with the aid of computers and accounting software. The technology is now cheap and easy to use.

Here we look at the advantages and limitations of using information technology for book-keeping and financial reporting.

Computerised accounting systems

There are a number of dedicated computerised accounting systems on the market including Sage, Pegasus, Tas, Quicken, Pacioli and many others. The most useful are integrated systems where the different sections of the ledger are linked so that a one-line entry automatically updates all relevant accounts.

Data entry

The normal procedure for entering data is:
- documents are sorted into batches – all invoices together, all cheques together, etc.
- transaction details are entered onto the appropriate screen. The double entry is carried out automatically using account codes. It is not necessary for the user to understand double entry book-keeping
- VAT is calculated by use of VAT codes

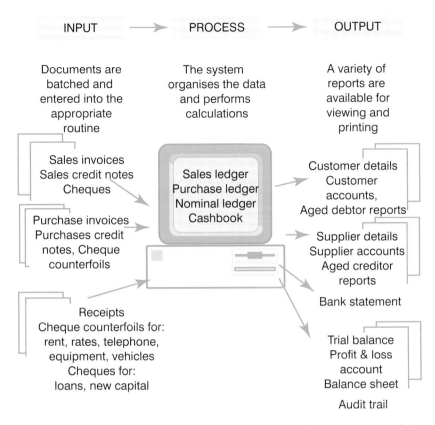

INPUT ⟶ PROCESS ⟶ OUTPUT

Documents are batched and entered into the appropriate routine

The system organises the data and performs calculations

A variety of reports are available for viewing and printing

Sales invoices
Sales credit notes
Cheques

Purchase invoices
Purchases credit notes, Cheque counterfoils

Receipts
Cheque counterfoils for:
rent, rates, telephone,
equipment, vehicles
Cheques for:
loans, new capital

Sales ledger
Purchase ledger
Nominal ledger
Cashbook

Customer details
Customer accounts,
Aged debtor reports

Supplier details
Supplier accounts
Aged creditor reports

Bank statement

Trial balance
Profit & loss account
Balance sheet
Audit trail

Figure 48 A computerised accounting system

- any data entered is automatically copied to each relevant part of the system. For instance a sales invoice entry will be posted to: the debtor's account, the sales account, the VAT account. All reports such as the trial balance, profit & loss account, balance sheet and aged debtor's report will be updated.

Figure 49 (page 88) shows how sales invoices would be entered.

Producing financial reports

Accounting packages are specialised databases. This means that any data that has been entered can be retrieved in a variety of formats. Reports can be produced instantly by clicking on the appropriate choice. Examples include:

- the audit trail (a list of all transactions)
- VAT return
- trial balance
- the profit & loss account and the balance sheet
- aged debtors and creditors reports, customer account details, bank account details, etc.
- graphs can be automatically generated to illustrate the figures
- new reports can be created and added to the list as required. These may include price lists which convert pounds sterling into foreign currencies.

Sage is an integrated package so that an entry to one part of the system will be automatically 'posted' to other relevant accounts. The Sage invoice screen acts like a day-book.

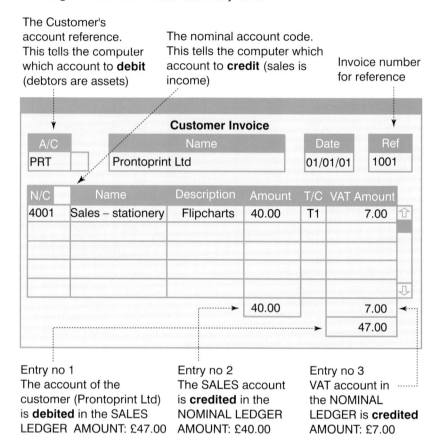

The Customer's account reference. This tells the computer which account to **debit** (debtors are assets)

The nominal account code. This tells the computer which account to **credit** (sales is income)

Invoice number for reference

Entry no 1
The account of the customer (Prontoprint Ltd) is **debited** in the SALES LEDGER AMOUNT: £47.00

Entry no 2
The SALES account is **credited** in the NOMINAL LEDGER AMOUNT: £40.00

Entry no 3
VAT account in the NOMINAL LEDGER is **credited** AMOUNT: £7.00

Figure 49 *Entering a sales invoice on the SAGE accounting package*

Solid Gold Pine Account Balances

A/C	Turnover	Credit Limit	Balance	Current	30 days	60 days	90 days	Older
Arfon & Griffiths	2,300.00	1,000.00	250.00	200.00	50.00	0.00	0.00	0.00
Colwyn & Co	3,650.00	1,000.00	550.00	0.00	0.00	500.00	50.00	0.00
Rock Relics Ltd	*5,320.00	500.00	600.00	600.00	0.00	0.00	0.00	0.00
St Davids Crafts	4,200.00	800.00	0.00	0.00	0.00	0.00	0.00	0.00
D Thomas	7,500.00	1,200.00	1,000.00	150.00	750.00	100.00	0.00	0.00
Totals	22,970.00	4,500.00	2,400.00	950.00	800.00	600.00	50.00	0.00

Figure 50 *An example of an aged debtors schedule*
Source: Format used by Sage Sterling's 'Financial Controller' accounting package

Notice that the computer has placed an asterisk against Rock Relic's account. What does this indicate?

Correcting errors

It is possible to correct errors and to delete entries. However, cancelled entries remain visible on the audit trail so that any change is apparent to the auditors; to allow users to remove all evidence of changes to entries would be to invite fraud.

Notice that the trial balance will always balance in a computerised system. This does not necessarily indicate that the accounts are correct, merely that the double entries have been carried out correctly. The package cannot check the data.

ACTIVITY

This trial balance was generated by a computerised accounting system.

	Debit			Credit
	£			£
Purchases	3,340		Sales	5,670
Bank	5,900		Creditors	130
Debtors	560		Vehicles	4,000
	9,800			9,800

Figure 51 *Example trial balance as at 31 December 200-*

Tasks

1 How do you know there is an error?
2 Why, despite an error, do the trial balance totals agree?
3 When the business bank statement arrived the finance manager had a shock. Why was this? What is the error likely to have been?

Other facilities

These may include:

- stock control and invoicing routines
- standard debt chasing letters which can automatically bring up customer details and outstanding balances if the account codes are inserted.

Statutory reports

The Inland Revenue and Customs and Excise will accept a floppy disk containing the data files from computerised accounting packages as an alternative to printed reports.

Advantages of computerised accounting:

- assuming that correct data and account codes are entered then the double entries and all of the balancing will be correct
- there is less keying in as each original entry is copied to all relevant files. This makes for speed and accuracy

- balances are immediately recalculated after each entry
- users do not need to learn double entry – this means that unskilled operators can produce accurate accounts
- corrections of errors are allowed
- there is automatic VAT calculation. Different VAT rates are available and can be updated as required
- there is rapid access to reports, for example, the aged debtors report, final accounts, VAT return, stock list, etc. Mail merge into standard letters and production of business documents is possible.

Disadvantages of using accounting software

Modern accounting software is inexpensive, easy to learn and extremely helpful. The most obvious disadvantages are those which apply to all software applications. These include:

- initial costs such as buying hardware and software, installation and staff training
- initial problems which may result from the need to input existing data from the manual system into the computer, 'teething' problems either with the system or with staff who are not yet proficient
- loss of data through virus, machine or disk error, operator error, power cuts, etc. Much of this can be avoided through keeping back-ups (preferably in a different location), keeping manual records or filing hard copy
- security – accounting data must be protected from the possibility of fraudulent use. For example, where data is on a network it may be possible for unauthorised users to 'hack' into the system. This may be avoided by a system of passwords to restrict access. Other common sense security measures include locking rooms, locking away disks and having visitors sign in to the building
- incompatibility – data stored on one system may not be easily recalled on another. This is a matter of good planning such as buying compatible software across the business from the start
- problems about whom to recruit. It is not necessary to understand double-entry book-keeping to use accounting software and a non-accountant might be cheaper to employ. However, this may lead to problems if the system is out of action such as staff failing to spot errors because the system always balances or staff having insufficient understanding to correct errors.

Legal restrictions on the use of computerised data

Where personal individual data is held on the computer it may become subject to the Data Protection Act of 1998, under which data subjects have rights of access to data held on them. Registration and administration can be onerous for businesses.

In fact this is not a major limitation of accounting software as data held for accounting purposes tends to be exempt from the Act. Relevant exemptions include:

- individuals who keep records on behalf of a club or voluntary organisation
- information which the law already requires a business to make public such as registered company members (shareholders)
- data maintained for payrolls, pensions and accounting purposes
- mailing lists, as long as the personal data only consists of names, addresses and other details needed for distribution such as phone numbers, fax numbers, e-mail addresses, etc.
- members' clubs (such as sports clubs), which are not registered companies – as long as members agree to the data being held.

CTIVITY

Use a book-keeping package to complete the accounts of The Music Shed for December.

Tasks

1 Set up customer accounts in the sales ledger.

Account	Lime & Co	West End	Big Bros
Code	LIM	Wes	BIG

2 Set up supplier accounts in the purchases ledger.

Account	AC Volt	Mike's Mikes Ltd
Code	ACV	MIK

Now enter the month's transactions in batches as follows:

3 Enter the purchases invoices for the month (VAT is at 17.5%).
Decide on the purchase account you will use (probably 5000 in SAGE).

Date	
3-Dec	AC Volt £720 + £126 VAT (invoice B/6520)
11-Dec	Mike's Mikes Ltd £4,000 + £700 VAT (invoice 7878)
18-Dec	Mike's Mikes Ltd £1,800 + £315 VAT (invoice 8222)

4 Enter the sales invoices for the month (VAT is at 17.5%).
Decide on the sales account you will use (probably 4000 in SAGE).

Date	
5-Dec	£1,200 + £210 VAT to Lime & Co (invoice 2000)
10-Dec	£4,000 + £700 VAT to West End (invoice 2001)
12-Dec	£2,200 + £385 VAT to West End (invoice 2002)
20-Dec	£1,400 + £245 VAT to Big Bros (invoice 2003)

5 Enter the purchases credit notes for the month.

Date
15-Dec   Mike's Mikes Ltd £640 + £112 VAT (credit note 881)
17-Dec   AC Volt £520 + £91 VAT (credit note BC/200)

6 Enter the sales credit notes for the month.

Date
16-Dec   West End £200 + £35 VAT (credit note C45)
19-Dec   Big Bros £360 + £63 VAT (credit note C46)

7 Enter the receipts from debtors and payments from creditors as follows. Decide which bank account you will use (probably 1200 in SAGE).

Date
5-Dec   Received a cheque for £2,400 from West End
24-Dec   Lime & Co settled their account by cheque
11-Dec   Paid AC Volt £3,500 by cheque

8 Enter the non-stock transactions to the bank account and nominal ledger (VAT is at 17.5% where applicable).
You will need to browse through to find the appropriate nominal account.

Date
1-Dec   Paid opening capital of £10,000 into the business
                bank account
2-Dec   Paid wages £45 (no VAT) by cheque
3-Dec   Paid for stationery £35 + VAT by cheque
7-Dec   Bought new office chairs for £1,250 + VAT by cheque
9-Dec   Paid electricity bill of £350 + VAT by cheque
14-Dec   Paid salaries £2,500 (no VAT) by cheque
17-Dec   Wrote a cheque for £45 (no VAT) to pay for travel
23-Dec   Paid £855 + VAT for advertising by cheque

9 Produce a trial balance, profit & loss account and a balance sheet (ignore closing stock). Also print out customer and supplier accounts.

10 Write a brief report to compare computerised and manual accounting methods. Use your experience and your wider knowledge to describe the advantages and limitations of using accounting software to produce accounts. Where possible supply examples to illustrate the points you make.

Appendix

World Cups: fully worked example – documents to trial balance

In the text we used the case study of World Cups to illustrate the various stages in the book-keeping process. The case study is restated here together with the solution. Transactions are grouped by type rather than date order, to fit with the text.

Receipts and payments (page 15)
- All items pass through the cash book (bank columns) with double entries to the ledger.
- For simplicity we assume there is no VAT.

Table A1 *Double entry example*

		Account debited	Account credited
01-May	Opened a business bank account by paying in £10,000 of savings	Bank	Capital
02-May	Paid rent of £1,000 by cheque	Rent	Bank
03-May	Bought a van for £2,000 paying by cheque	Van	Bank
04-May	Bought stock for £600 paying by cheque	Purchases	Bank
05-May	Sold stock for £1,800 with payment by cheque	Bank	Sales
06-May	Raised a loan of £500	Bank	Loan
07-May	Bought more stock for £400 by cheque	Purchases	Bank

Credit sales, credit purchases and returns (pages 9–11)
Here document details are recorded in the appropriate day book. The way to complete a double entry is to:
- enter each document total to the appropriate customer or supplier account
- enter day book totals to the general ledger at the end of the month.

Table A2 *Credit sales*

		Account debited	Account credited
08-May	£160+ £28 VAT to JJ Ltd (invoice 600)	JJ Ltd	
15-May	£200 + £35 to B & B (invoice 601)	B & B	Sales and VAT – using monthly day book totals**
22-May	£40 + £ VAT to Patel & Co (invoice 602)	Patel & Co	
26-May	£440 + £77 VAT to B Cotton (invoice 603)	B Cotton	

Table A3 *Credit purchases*

		Account debited	Account credited
09-May	£280 + £49 VAT from Wilson Bros (invoice W967)	Purchases and VAT – using monthly day book totals**	Wilson Bros
12-May	£180 + £31.50 VAT from KGB (invoice 997)		KGB
24-May	£60 + £10.50 VAT from Ahmed Ltd (invoice AL34)		Ahmed Ltd

Table A4 *Sales returns*

		Account debited	Account credited
17-May	£16 + £2.80 VAT from JJ Ltd (credit note C10)	Sales returns and VAT – using monthly day book totals**	JJ Ltd
19-May	£64 + £11.20 VAT from B & B (credit note C11)		KGB

Table A5 *Purchase returns*

		Account debited	Account credited
08-May	£8 + £1.40 VAT to KGB (credit note C05)	KGB	Purchase returns and VAT – using monthly day book totals**
29-May	£32 + £5.60 VAT to Ahmed Ltd (credit note CA12)	Ahmed Ltd	
31-May	All day books are totalled and the totals transferred to the general ledger**.		
	All accounts are balanced with balances brought down to 1 June.		
	A trial balance is prepared to check the accuracy of the ledger.		

Day books

Table A6 Sales day book

Date	Details	Invoice No	Total (excl VAT)	VAT	Total (incl VAT)
8-May	JJ Ltd	600	160.00	28.00	188.00
15-May	B & B	601	200.00	35.00	235.00
22-May	Patel & Co	602	40.00	7.00	47.00
26-May	B Cotton	603	440.00	77.00	517.00
31-May	Total (to general ledger)		840.00	147.00	

Table A7 Returns inwards (sales returns) day book

Date	Details	Credit Note No	Total (excl VAT)	VAT	Total (incl VAT)
17-May	JJ Ltd	C10	16.00	2.80	18.80
19-May	B & B	C11	64.00	11.20	75.20
31-May	Total (to general ledger)		80.00	14.00	

Table A8 Purchases day book

Date	Details	Invoice No	Total (excl VAT)	VAT	Total (incl VAT)
9-May	Wilson Bros	W967	280.00	49.00	329.00
12-May	KGB	997	180.00	31.50	211.50
24-May	Ahmed Ltd	AL34	60.00	10.50	70.50
31-May	Total (to general ledger)		520.00	91.00	

Table A9 Returns outwards (purchases returns) day book

Date	Details	Credit Note No	Total (excl VAT)	VAT	Total (incl VAT)
18-May	KGB	C05	8.00	1.40	9.40
29-May	Ahmed Ltd	CA12	32.00	5.60	37.60
31-May	Total (to general ledger)		40.00	7.00	

Figure A1 *Cash book*

Cash book (Bank columns only)

1-May	Capital	10,000	2-May	Rent	1,000
5-May	Sales	1,800	3-May	Van	2,000
6-May	Loan	500	4-May	Purchases	600
			7-May	Purchases	400
			7-May	Balance c/d	8,300
		12,300			12,300
1-Jun	Balance b/d	8,300			

Figure A2 *General ledger*

Capital

7-May	Balance c/d	10,000	1-May	Bank	10,000
			1-Jun	Balance b/d	10,000

Rent

2-May	Bank	1,000	7-May	Balance c/d	1,000
1-Jun	Balance b/d	1,000			

Van

3-May	Bank	2,000	7-May	Balance c/d	2,000
1-Jun	Balance b/d	2,000			

Loan

31-May	Balance c/d	500	6-May	Bank	500
			1-Jun	Balance b/d	500

VAT

31-May	Sales returns DB	14	31-May	Sales DB	147
31-May	Purchases DB	91	31-May	Purchase	7
31-May	Balance c/d	49		Returns DB	
		154			154
			1-Jun	Balance b/d	49

Sales

			5-May	Bank	1,800
31-May	Balance c/d	2,640	31-May	Sales DB	840
		2,640			2,640
			1-Jun	Balance b/d	2,640

Cont'd

Sales returns

31-May	Sales returns DB	80	31-May Balance c/d	80
1-Jun	Balance b/d	80		

Purchases

4-May	Bank	600		
7-May	Bank	400		
31-May	Purchases DB	520	7-May Balance c/d	1,520
		1,520		1,520
1-Jun	Balance b/d	1,520		

Purchase returns

31-May	Balance c/d	40	31-May Purchase returns DB	40
			1-Jun Balance b/d	40

Figure A3 *Sales ledger (Customer/debtor accounts)*

JJ Ltd

8-May	Sales	188.00	17-May Sales returns	18.80
			31-May Balance c/d	169.20
		188.00		188.00
1-Jun	Balance b/d	169.20		

B & B

15-May	Sales	235.00	19-May Sales returns	75.20
			31-May Balance c/d	159.80
		235.00		235.00
1-Jun	Balance b/d	159.80		

Patel & Co

22-May	Sales	47.00	31-May Balance c/d	47.00
1-Jun	Balance b/d	47.00		

B Cotton

31-May	Sales	517.00	31-May Balance c/d	517.00
1-Jun	Balance b/d	517.00		

Figure A4 *Purchases ledger (Supplier/creditor accounts)*

Wilson Bros

31-May Balance c/d	329.00	9-May Purchases		329.00
		1-Jun Balance b/d		329.00

KGB

18-May Purchase returns	9.40	12-May Purchases		211.50
31-May Balance c/d	202.10			
	211.50			211.50
		1-Jun Balance b/d		202.10

Ahmed Ltd

29-May Purchase returns	37.60	24-May Purchases		70.50
31-May Balance c/d	32.90			
	70.50			70.50
		1-Jun Balance b/d		32.90

Figure A5 *Trial balance as at 31st May 200-*

	Debit	Credit
	£	£
Bank	8,300	
Capital		10,000
Rent	1,000	
Van	2,000	
Loan		500
VAT		49
Purchases	1,520	
Sales		2,640
Purchase returns		40
Sales returns	80	
Debtors	893	
Creditors		564
	13,793	13,793

	Trial balance		Adjustments		Trading and profit & loss		Balance sheet	
	Dr £	Cr £	Dr £	Cr £	Dr £	Cr £	Dr £	Cr £
Sales		414,250				414,250		
Opening stock	70,000				70,000			
Purchases	275,500				275,500			
Heating and lighting	14,750		350		15,100			
Salaries	36,600			400	36,200			
Post and packaging	1,400				1,400			
Insurance	3,800			250	3,550			
Advertising	3,400		765		4,165			
Premises	120,000						120,000	
Fixtures and fittings (at cost)	45,000						45,000	
Provision for depreciation – fixtures and fittings		9,000		4,500				13,500
Debtors	55,000						55,000	
Bank	9,000						9,000	
Creditors		47,000						47,000
Opening capital		195,000						195,000
Mortgage		4,200						4,200
Drawings	35,000						35,000	
	669,450	669,450						
Closing stock – profit & loss account				60,000		60,000		
Closing stock – balance sheet			60,000				60,000	
Salaries prepaid – balance sheet			400				400	
Insurance prepaid – balance sheet			250				250	
Heating and lighting due – balance sheet				350				350
Advertising due – balance sheet				765				765
Depreciation – fixtures and fittings profit & loss account			4,500		4,500			
Net profit					63,835			63,835
			66,265	66,265	474,250	474,250	324,650	324,650

An accountant may use an extended trial balance (or worksheet) to help in preparing the final accounts.

Here each figure on the trial balance is extended into either the trading and profit & loss account column or the balance sheet column as appropriate. Notice that debits are extended as debits and credits as credits.

Any adjustments are listed in the adjustments column. Notice that for each there is a debit and a credit entry. The first entry is next to the item on the trial balance.

Figure A6 Extended trial balance of Southwark Supplies as at 31 December 200-(see page 52)

Index